This Book is Presented to

_____

By

_____

On the Date of

_____

BAPTISM
IN THE
SPIRIT

STANFORD E. LINZEY, JR., D.MIN.
CAPTAIN, CHAPLAIN CORPS, UNITED STATES NAVY, RETIRED

BAPTISM
IN THE
SPIRIT

For All People of All Faiths

FOREWORD BY
STANLEY M. HORTON, TH.D.

EDITED BY
JAMES F. LINZEY, D.D. & VERNA M. LINZEY, D.D.

MILITARY BIBLE ASSOCIATION
ESCONDIDO, CALIFORNIA

Unless otherwise indicated, all Bible quotations are taken from the King James Version of the Bible, replacing 'Holy Ghost' with 'Holy Spirit.'

ISBN: 978-1936857-06-7

Library of Congress Control Number: 2011962448

COMMENTS

"Gentlemen, if you are going to be a spiritual leader, you need a spiritual experience. This book leads the way."

GENERAL RALPH E. HAINES, JR., UNITED STATES ARMY, RETIRED
(CONTINENTAL ARMY COMMANDER)

"There is a tie that binds today's Sailors and Marines with those who went before us, and that is the fierce devotion to service – service to our nation, service to our Navy, and service to our Shipmates. It remains the underlying theme of military life, a belief that we are part of something much greater than any one person. Your dedication to that ideal was never more evident than it was at the Battle of Midway in June 1942…. On behalf of the men and women of our Navy, thank you for your service and best wishes for success in all of life's adventures."

ADMIRAL VERN CLARK, UNITED STATES NAVY, RETIRED
CHIEF OF NAVAL OPERATIONS
(BATTLE OF MIDWAY ANNIVERSARY)

"Admiral Chester Nimitz said that 'it is the function of the Navy to carry the war to the enemy so that it will not be fought on U.S. soil.'… Though there were still years of difficult fighting ahead, your victory at Midway dealt our enemy a blow from which it would not recover…We draw strength from the example set by you… While the debt of gratitude we owe you can never be repaid, we want you to know that we are working every day to protect America and live up to the legacy of courage and commitment you forged at Midway. We salute you, and we wish you all the best."

ADMIRAL TIMOTHY J. KEATING, UNITED STATES NAVY
NORTH AMERICAN AEROSPACE DEFENSE COMMAND
AND UNITED STATES NORTHERN COMMAND
(63RD ANNIVERSARY OF THE BATTLE OF MIDWAY)

"Thank you for your service to our country. Today's Navy would not be the same without your contribution."

VICE ADMIRAL J.M. ZORTMAN, UNITED STATES NAVY
COMMANDER, NAVAL AIR FORCES
(VICTORY AT MIDWAY COMMEMORATION)

"The world saw fire in the upper room and stood back in fear. This book will ignite the fire of God in your heart and you will never be the same. *Baptism in the Spirit* by Stanford E. Linzey, Jr., is a book every true believer must read for spiritual empowerment."

GENERAL KINGSLEY BENJAMIN, CHAPLAIN CORPS, REPUBLIC OF NIGERIA ARMY
PENTECOSTAL

"Our congregation is still resounding with the praise of God resulting from your message on the baptism in the Holy Spirit."

CHAPLAIN (COLONEL) SCOTT MCCHRYSTAL, USA, (RET.)
MILITARY/VETERANS' ADMINISTRATION REPRESENTATIVE & ENDORSER
ASSEMBLIES OF GOD CHAPLAINCY MINISTRIES
(STATEMENT TO CAPTAIN STANFORD E. LINZEY, JR., OCTOBER 24, 1989)

"'…show hospitality to strangers, for thereby some have entertained angels unawares' (Hebrews 13:2, RSV). Stan Linzey the 'stranger' entered my life on a dreary Wednesday morning in 1968 in the Bureau of Naval Personnel (BUPERS) Admiral's dining room, where I had perfunctorily gone to a prayer breakfast. After wallowing all night on the floor of my home in Arlington, VA, weeping over John 14:12-15 and my inability to witness or to 'take a stand for Christ,' I was exhausted, barely interested in breakfast, but not the least interested in 'strangers.' The stranger then rose from the breakfast table and announced that 'The Holy Spirit just told me to read you a Scripture.' In terror I fell on my knees, because I knew what Scripture the stranger was going to read: John 14:12-15. Stan Linzey, whom I found out later was the stranger, then laid his hands on my head. His hands became like branding irons, and my head "burned" day and night for two weeks with their imprint. I began to speak or pray in another language, and began to see souls saved—privates and sergeants, at least one general, and one admiral, and my own German-Jew mother and Scottish alcoholic dad. Stan Linzey, from my perspective, certainly was an 'angel'—a messenger from God. "

COLONEL MYRL ALLINDER, USMC-RET.

"What an inspiring book! For here you learn from Scripture and the testimonies of others how to become a New Testament Christian. Filled with the Spirit, you are now empowered and equipped to accomplish all that God has called and destined you to be and do."

CAPTAIN DAVID PLANK, CHC, USN (RET.)
UNITED CHURCH OF CHRIST

"In reading this book of sermons, *Baptism in the Spirit*, I have felt like I have actually been with my friend of over fifty years, Stan Linzey. These sermons are Stan, his forcefulness, his disarming humor, his use of Scripture to support his teaching. I met Stan in 1958. I had reported to my first assignment as a Navy Chaplain at Camp Pendleton. I became the third Assemblies of God minister to receive a regular commission as a Navy Chaplain and the second to attain the rank of Captain. The Division Chaplain at Pendleton knew Chaplain Linzey and suggested that he would be a good model for me to visit and learn from in beginning my work as a Chaplain. Stan was stationed at the Naval Training Center in San Diego. I visited him there, and we have been friends ever since. We have had some similar experiences, served at different times at some of the same commands, were in the same senior course in Newport, Rhode Island in 1970. Both of us attended a variety of colleges and seminaries, including a year at Harvard Divinity School. But Stan Linzey is one unique individual. There is only one Stan Linzey.

"I mentioned Stan's forcefulness. An example is found in this book. A Marine had said to him, 'I'm not even saved.' Chaplain Linzey said, 'Then get saved!' He did and was baptized with the Spirit. Chaplain Linzey commented, 'Like I tell you about Marines, when you command them to get saved, they do! Hallelujah!' When he told Sailors and Marines to be in chapel, they came. He filled chapels that way, won converts that way, impressed commands that way. He even said, 'Receive the Holy Spirit!' that way, and thousands did. At the senior course, someone decided we shouldn't keep the same seats in class. Some were asking others to move so that they could have that seat. One Chaplain asked Stan Linzey to protect him from this moving. Big forceful Stan stood behind him, and no one was going to make his smaller friend move.

"I said that Stan Linzey was unique. His preaching and writing and ministry on receiving the baptism of the Holy Spirit have no equal of which I am aware. He lets you know exactly what he believes and carefully shows the Scriptural basis, even when a casual reading isn't adequate. He looks at every time in Acts that people received the baptism in the Spirit and establishes that they spoke in tongues. I hope this book will be widely read."

CAPTAIN MARVIN E. SNYDER, CHC, USN (RET.)
ASSEMBLIES OF GOD

"Reading this manuscript brought back many memories of Stan Linzey. As I read it, I can just hear Stan speaking."

CAPTAIN STANLEY D. MILLER, CHC, USN (RET.)
UNITED CHURCH OF CHRIST

"It was a real pleasure for me to serve at the same time as Captain Stanford Linzey. God showed me favor by allowing me to have such a friend as he. He was a wonderful person. I always admired Captain Linzey for his ministry and work on the Holy Spirit. All through Stan's military career he always emphasized in word, in deed, in sermons and books, and in his way of life the preeminence of the Holy Spirit and its importance for Christians today. I am delighted to add my comment to the work of this man of God who served God and country with all of his might. *Baptism in the Spirit* is what Captain Stanford Linzey was all about. I highly recommend it."

CHAPLAIN, COLONEL, LEMUEL D. MCELYEA, USAF (RET.)
FORMER ENDORSER, COMMISSION ON CHAPLAINS,
ASSEMBLIES OF GOD

"I have read Captain Stanford E. Linzey's sermons and was totally blessed with his honesty and his humor. It was refreshing to know that he believed very much like I do and that he had a very interesting way of presenting his views. I had the joy and privilege of meeting Captain Linzey when he visited the United States Army Reserve Command in Atlanta, GA. He was a very easy individual to talk with. I enjoyed hearing about his experiences in the Navy during World War II. It was a joy and pleasure to read his sermons and I believe this book will be a blessing to all who will have the opportunity to read it."

CHAPLAIN (COLONEL) ROB NOLAND, USAR (RET.)
FORMER DEPUTY COMMAND CHAPLAIN, UNITED STATES ARMY RESERVE
COMMAND
INTERNATIONAL CHURCH OF THE FOURSQUARE GOSPEL

"In November 1971, I came on board the USS *Coral Sea* as a Seaman attached to VA-94. I had just turned 24 years old and I was wondering what in the world was I doing by going on this WESTPAC Combat Cruise to Vietnam. Little did I know that God had a plan. There was a Senior Chaplain on board the USS *Coral Sea* by the name of Commander Stan Linzey. Later he was promoted to Captain. He was an Assembly of God Chaplain and he was so kind and pastoral in his ministry and service to the men on board ship during that cruise. On January 20, 1972, I was invited by another seaman, 3rd Class Petty Officer Frank Klapach to have a meeting with Chaplain Linzey to discuss the baptism of the Holy Spirit and speaking in other tongues. Later, this 3rd Class petty Officer became Chaplain Frank Klapach. I accepted that invitation. Chaplain Linzey asked me if I knew Jesus as my personal Lord and Savior. I had previously met the Lord Jesus Christ and had a born again experience on 3 April 1971. I said to Chaplain Linzey, 'Yes, I know the Lord as my personal Lord and Savior.' He then began telling me about the baptism of the Holy Spirit and speaking in other tongues. In his teaching and scriptural references he was very clear and articulate. It was very helpful for me to hear this message presented to me. Chaplain Linzey then asked me if I would be interested in receiving this gift. I said, 'Well, I believe that this is from God. And I believe God wants to give it to people. But does God want me to receive this gift personally?' Chaplain Linzey was very kind and patient. He turned to Romans 8:26 and quoted this verse: 'Likewise the Spirit also helps in our weaknesses. For we do not know what we should pray for as we ought, but the Spirit Himself makes intercessions for us with groanings which cannot be uttered.' 'Jim,' Chaplain Linzey said, 'that means that it is for you. Do you want to receive?' I said, 'Yes.' Chaplain Linzey and Frank Klapach laid hands on me and I began speaking in a language that I had never learned before. It was as if Someone had reached His hand down my throat and pulled that language out. It was like honey pouring out of my mouth. It was a very sweet, non-emotional encounter with God that I shall never forget. Chaplain Linzey was used by the Lord to lead many people into the fullness of the baptism of the Holy Spirit and speak in other tongues. I am thankful that I was one of them."

CHAPLAIN, LT. COL. JAMES HOUGH, USAF (RET.)
INTERNATIONAL CHURCH OF THE FOURSQUARE GOSPEL
(ONE OF THE THREE ROMAN CATHOLIC SAILORS ON THE USS CORAL SEA WHO
RECEIVED THE BAPTISM WITH THE HOLY SPIRIT UNDER CHAPLAIN LINZEY'S
MINISTRY AND BECAME A PENTECOSTAL MILITARY CHAPLAIN)

"*Baptism in the Spirit* is a controversial subject. The enemy knows that when the church gets a revelation of the power and impact of the Holy Spirit, his defeat will be reinforced in a greater way. Captain Stanford E. Linzey, Jr., CHC, USN (Ret), provides a powerful summary of the nuances of the Holy Spirit. This is the book to read for a greater understanding and application of the Holy Spirit in your life and church."

CHAPLAN (LTC) PEARLEAN SCOTT, USA (RET.)
FORMER COMMAND CHAPLAIN, U.S. ARMY CADET COMMAND
ASSEMBLIES OF GOD INTERNATIONAL FELLOWSHIP

"There is something extra special about my friend Stan who inspired me with his acumen as a minister of ministers. This is especially true in the way he presented himself as God's representative while leading so many of us into a better understanding by his knowledge and experience in the special ministry of the infilling of the Holy Spirit. I first met and became acquainted with Stan when we were both students in Bible College. He was a serviceman fresh out of the navy and had assumed the pastorate of a small church in El Cajon, CA. I was a recent Air Force pilot retiree and still in service of the Air Force Reserve. I had acquired a turkey ranch a few miles out of town. The commonality of our backgrounds made the way to bond our friendship. That friendship never lost its meaning after we both went though training at the same institutions and on into our fields of service in the Lord's harvest. I was a Baptist deacon in a nearby church, and Stan had invited me to speak to his young people one Wednesday night. After that service I was never the same. It was the practice to have a prayer session around the altar after the preaching, so I found a space on the piano bench. Everyone was praising, praying or seeking more of the Spirit. Suddenly, I was impressed to recall a Bible verse in Mt. 27:46 where Jesus cried out in a loud voice, 'Eli, Eli. Lama sabachthani.' And at the same moment my voice began uttering sounds of praise and honor in tongues to our Lord! Yes, I became a Pentecostal Baptist that night. The one thing I did hear and remember was THE SHOUT OF VICTORY by Brother Linzey: 'Chinn has the baptism!' I know it was the fruit of his and the Linzey family's prayers that helped to bring that experience into fruition. So many untold numbers have been enriched in their lives by this man's ministry through his books and testimony. That ministry brings a smile from heaven of what this soldier of the cross has meant to the cause of Christ and to so many of His worker's lives. We have only one life, and it will soon be past, but only what is done for Christ will last!"

CHAPLAIN, LT. COL. JACK J. CHINN, USAF (RET.)
PENTECOSTAL CHURCH OF GOD

"Stan Linzey was an irrepressible minister of the gospel. He presented his understanding of the Pentecostal distinctives with humor and gusto. His unique personality radiates through these sermons."

COMMANDER R. GLENN BROWN, CHC, USN (RET.)
ASSEMBLIES OF GOD

"Chaplain Stan Linzey hit it right on the head. He reaffirmed everything I know about the baptism and taught me a couple of new things I didn't know. It was a joy to read and really re-invigorated my desire to pray in the Spirit more! Chaplain Linzey has captured both the simplicity and profundity of God's Word, pertaining to the baptism with the Holy Spirit. His book 'kicks over' every sacred cow of legalism and denominationalism that has prevented people from understanding the place, power, and purpose for the baptism with the Holy Spirit in every Christian's life. I agree with him. I wish every person in the world could read this book."

LTC Howard L. Malone, USA (Ret.)
Former Chief, Combined Security Transition Command Headquarters
Afghanistan

"Stan served for many years as Chaplain for the Hidden Valley Chapter (Escondido, California) of the Retired Officers Association. His invocations and benedictions were always inspirational and topical. He touched people in a way that few are able and I always felt moved in his presence. I miss him."

LTC Harry A. Hodges, USA (Ret.)
President, Hidden Valley Chapter
Military Officers Association

"I returned to faith in Christ because my wife became a Christian. This was in Cyprus in 1980. She was frightened because she attended a prayer meeting where an army cook prayed out loud in 'Tongues'. She begged me to come with her and if necessary protect her from this madman! Being an ex-Royal Marine and now a serving RAF intelligence 'gatherer' I believed I could handle the situation! Truth was that I was puzzled and quite liked this group. The chaplain was a British Army major. Massive guy, big rugby player. He and I hit it off well together. Truth was, looking back now this was the start of a revival. The chaplain loaned me a tape of a Southern Baptist preacher teaching on the Baptism of the Holy Spirit. At the end of listening to the tape the preacher said, 'use it or loose it' with regard to speaking in tongues. Blow me I spoke forth, all on my own, and was speaking in tongues. I couldn't stop myself! Now this revival took off. The predominantly Anglican (Church of England) and military garrison congregation became fired up for Christ. The poor old chaplain didn't know what to do! But with all things in the military, time and people move on and we all parted company. But the fire had been lit. Many of the folk went on into all sorts of mission fields. God knows how many people have heard the gospel through us all. The garrison Sergeant Major left the army and became an Anglican Priest! Stan Linzey's book? I wish I could have read it back then. It would have helped us all. He must have been a real down to earth sort of guy. What he teaches has a great deal to do with his experience and putting his faith into practice. He tells you what he experienced and doesn't pull any punches. I'm sure you will be edified and illuminated by his style. He certainly knows his Hebrew and Greek and it shows. What he has written is easy to understand, even for an Englishman like me. I sure do wish I had been able to read this book when I was starting out in my ministry. But never to late, I'm sure the Lord will remind me of it as I continue!"

MAJOR ROBERT LUCAS, RAF (RET.), UNITED KINGDOM
CHAPLAIN, ROYAL AIR FORCE ASSOCIATION
BAPTIST

"I was gripped by *Baptism in the Spirit*. Captain Stanford Linzey was a most intensive minister of the Lord. His professional command of Scripture was commendable, and clearly, his work was inspired by the Holy Spirit. This man of God touched the lives of all whom he met and changed their lives forever. He was blessed to be anointed by the Holy Spirit. His work lives on."

CHAPLAIN (CPT) WILLIAM C. BARON, USAR
EASTERN ORTHODOX

"Dr. Stanford Linzey Jr. was a true pioneer in the Classical Pentecostal movement. I experienced first hand the mighty move of God that was exhibited through his ministry. I was a sailor on the USS *Coral Sea* (CVA-43) during the 1971-72 cruise which served off the coast of Vietnam. God moved in a mighty way and several of us became full time clergy and military chaplains. I commend his work to anyone who is hungry for God."

FORMER CHAPLAIN (CPT) MICHAEL PACELLA, III, USA
CHARISMATIC EPISCOPAL
(ONE OF THE THREE ROMAN CATHOLIC SAILORS ON THE USS CORAL SEA WHO
RECEIVED THE BAPTISM WITH THE HOLY SPIRIT UNDER CHAPLAIN LINZEY'S
MINISTRY AND BECAME A PENTECOSTAL MILITARY CHAPLAIN)

"I have been proud of my Uncle Stan and Aunt Verna my whole life. I have told Captain Linzey's story to many of my friends—how he and his prayer group were spared in the murky waters before the USS *Yorktown* sank in the Battle of Midway during World War II. Their ministry on the baptism with the Holy Spirit began when Captain Linzey was a sailor in the military and it flourished throughout their lives. This book contains those historic messages. It will inspire all who read it."

SGT. DENNIS A. HALL, SR., USMC-RET.
CHAPLAIN, VETERANS OF FOREIGN WARS, POST 9400, PHOENIX, ARIZONA

"Having served aboard the USS *Galveston* in 1967, we deployed for a Mediterranean Cruise. Chaplain Stanford E. Linzey, Jr., was the chaplain at that time and I attended the services aboard ship. I have so many wonderful memories of that 1967 cruise."

FORMER SEAMAN KENNETH J. RUIZ, USN
USS GALVESTON
ROMAN CATHOLIC

"God sent to planet earth this common man with God-given talents to preach an uncommon message. Through continuous, in-depth, theological preparation, Captain Stanford E. Linzey, Jr., expanded his evangelical mission by spreading far across the miles the Good News of the Word of God and the power of the Holy Spirit. His Navy career proved to be fertile ground for discipleship—encouragement to the believing sailor and inspiration to the unbelieving sailor—as they prepared to battle enemies at sea. This library of sermons is testimony and a legacy of a man's love of and dedication to God and how he reached out to meet the spiritual needs of others. God bless him, all those whose lives have been touched by him, and the loving editors of *Baptism in the Spirit*."

LOIS DEBORDE
USS YORKTOWN (CV-5) CLUB

"The raw Captain Stan Linzey—what he said and how he said it! This book will keep you up all night. We highly recommend it."

MILITARY BIBLE ASSOCIATION

"Captain Stan Linzey eloquently articulates the awesome privilege given to believers to receive the baptism of the Holy Spirit. His in-depth synopsis of the various dispensations accent the necessity of our post-modern society to be refreshed, realigned, and engaged in teaching the significance and benefits of having the indwelling presence of the living God. Certainly, if we as a nation would return to these basic biblical principles, the world would see innumerable and powerful demonstrations of God in the earth."

DR. JANICE HOLLIS
FORMER CANDIDATE, LIEUTENANT GOVERNOR, PENNSYLVANIA

"An exciting handbook on the Holy Spirit...a bridge-builder between old-time Pentecostals and those who are fresh in the Spirit from all other backgrounds."

PAT BOONE
INTERNATIONAL CHURCH OF THE FOURSQUARE GOSPEL
(COMMENT FOR PENTECOST IN THE PENTAGON, WHICH WAS BASED ON THESE SERMONS)

"I believe as you read U.S. Navy Chaplain Stanford E. Linzey's book, you'll feel the gripping power of Stanford Linzey's "action" in the heat of battle all over this planet. As he powerfully tells us now, you'll be transformed to the roots of your being, as I was. Captain Linzey spiritually and literally moved in the power of the Holy Spirit baptism, relying on "prayer language of the Holy Spirit" and his native tongue. I believe you won't put the book down. It will lift you into a new dimension of facing life with the power of the Holy Spirit baptism. You're about to be greatly blessed."

ORAL ROBERTS
UNITED METHODIST
(COMMENT FOR THE HOLY SPIRIT IN THE THIRD MILLENNIUM, WHICH WAS BASED ON THESE SERMONS)

"Captain Stanford E. Linzey, Jr.'s *Baptism in the Spirit: For All People of All Faiths* is informative and invigorating. I particularly enjoyed its fresh, user-friendly approach. Based on a sermon series on the Classical Pentecostal doctrine of Spirit baptism, this book casts a wide net, making it ecumenical in the best sense of the word—as the subtitle itself clearly declares—while remaining anchored in the author's own Pentecostal tradition. Filled with dramatic testimonies and infused with delightful humor, this study also fairly but straightforwardly addresses questions many non-Pentecostal people ask about the Pentecostal experience and accompanying manifestations such as speaking in tongues and other spiritual gifts and demonstrations. Along the way, Linzey good-naturedly debunks prevalent misconceptions in a sort of Pentecostal demythologization process. However, this text is written in understandable and, not infrequently, entertaining language. A particular distinctive of this popular level text is its willingness to draw on multidisciplinary insights while maintaining a staunchly biblical foundation and framework. Carefully interwoven with achievements from Linzey's admirable military and ministerial career, the posthumous publication of this book is a fitting tribute to its author. Perhaps most importantly, it offers helpful advice and instruction for those seeking to understand and/or experience Holy Spirit baptism as well as for those wishing to learn more about living and walking in the Spirit subsequently. May God grant it to be so! Amen."

TONY RICHIE, D.MIN, PH.D.
THE PNEUMA REVIEW

"At a time when there seems to be a decreasing emphasis on the baptism in the Holy Spirit in many of our Pentecostal churches, this book not only offers a solid doctrinal examination of the Scriptures, it also provides practical experience gained from a life devoted to Christ and leading people into the baptism in the Holy Spirit. I pray that God will use this book to stir up hearts and ignite a passion for the fullness of the Spirit."

REV. GEORGE EKEROTH
EXECUTIVE DIRECTOR
ASSEMBLIES OF GOD INTERNATIONAL FELLOWSHIP

"The legacy of the life of Stanford Linzey is typified in the release of this mighty and masterful work on the Baptism in the Spirit. Revd. Captain Stanford Linzey was simply a man's man, a navy man, but more importantly than all of this was his deep and profound love of God. Like his life during the 'earthly living years' this literary work will have its wonderful effect on so many more, reaching them and encouraging them to stretch forth themselves into the deeper things of the Lord's eternal blessings for all of us."

REV. DR. STEPHEN J. HOUSTON
PRESIDENT, WORLD CONFERENCE OF INDEPENDENT METHODIST CHURCHES
UNITED KINGDOM

"Stan offers a spirited and engaging collection of sermons spanning the range of Old and New Testament teachings on Spirit-baptism from a classical Pentecostal perspective. From his vast experience and legacy as an Assemblies of God Navy chaplain, he dispels many of the errant beliefs and practices often associated with fringe Pentecostalism. Yet he also conveys sage guidance and direction regarding the biblically rooted and genuinely experiential dynamic of being filled with the Holy Spirit and speaking in tongues. Simply read, enjoy and be truly inspired as was I."

RAY RACHELS
FORMER DISTRICT SUPERINTENDENT
SOUTHERN CALIFORNIA ASSEMBLIES OF GOD

"Chaplain Stanford E. Linzey has been mightily used of God to instruct, inspire and lead countless believers into the baptism of the Holy Spirit as evidenced by the presence of a language of the Spirit. Using his great grasp of Scripture, his understanding of the ways of God, and his sensitivity to the need in believers' lives for Spirit fullness, Chaplain Linzey has been used of the Lord to help believers move past denominational and personal barriers into a new encounter with the dynamic of Spirit baptism. Here is a collection of messages from Chaplain Linzey which represent the richness of his teaching ministry. You will be blessed and challenged as you journey with him into the marvelous life of the Spirit."

RICHARD L. DRESSELHAUS, D.MIN.
EXECUTIVE PRESBYTER, SOUTHWEST REGION
GENERAL COUNCIL OF THE ASSEMBLIES OF GOD

"I will always remember the services you held for us in Manteca."

DONALD E. ANNAS
DISTRICT SUPERINTENDENT,
NORTHERN CALIFORNIA-NEVADA DISTRICT COUNCIL OF THE
ASSEMBLIES OF GOD,
MARCH 1, 1993

"What a Victory! What a Blessing! Our Holy Spirit Crusade was wonderful. Your clear Bible messages helped many to understand how to receive the Holy Spirit. The Revival is continuing. We want to thank you for coming and ministering to our people. Your message was truly a blessing from the Lord. In the days ahead we all need a more clear understanding of the Holy Spirit's power in our daily lives. We are looking forward with great anticipation to your next visit with us. Again, thank you for your ministry to our people."

R. KENNETH GEORGE
PASTOR, FIRST ASSEMBLY OF GOD
ALBUQUERQUE, NEW MEXICO
JUNE 5, 1992

"Westminster Assembly was moved upon by the Holy Spirit through his messages. As a senior pastor with many years of experience, it is always refreshing to have guest preachers who are intellectually and educationally qualified to dig in the profound depths of Scriptural truth… The Chaplain's unique approach to the fullness of the Baptism with the Holy Spirit has a disarming affect upon many people who have struggled to receive."

RUBEN A. WILSON
SENIOR PASTOR, WESTMINSTER ASSEMBLY
SEATTLE, WASHINGTON
SEPTEMBER 17, 1986

"WOW! This is the word that the church, here in Elsinore, is using to describe the fantastic move of God that we experienced during your time with us. During your meetings we had 142 receive the Baptism with Spirit and many were healed and several saved… Brother Linzey, you are truly a man anointed of god for such a time as this. The message that God has given you, and the method in which you deliver that Word is made simple enough so that anyone, even children, can understand it and receive it's worth… Thank you for being a real blessing to this Pastor and this flock. We will look forward to another great time of ministry and fellowship with you soon."

FRED R. RODRIQUEZ
SENIOR PASTOR, FIRST ASSEMBLY OF GOD CHURCH
LAKE ELSINORE, CALIFORNIA
JULY 27, 1992

"I so much appreciated your ministry to the congregation here at First Assembly Sunday morning. It was such a blessing to our hearts. Brother Linzey, God has certainly anointed your ministry. The way that you present "the manifestation of the Holy Spirit" makes it so much easier for many of our people to understand, and to accept all that the Lord has for them. I was thrilled with the results of your message Sunday morning—with 18 of those present obtaining the fullness of the Spirit, with the evidence of speaking in tongues."

KEN JONES
PASTOR, FIRST ASSEMBLY OF GOD
CLEBURNE, TEXAS
AUGUST 6, 1985

"I have learned more about what Pentecost is, the blessings of Pentecost, and the benefits of Pentecost, from the preaching of Brother Linzey than from all the books I have read. I was thrilled by his explanation of the psychological benefits of speaking in tongues, the therapeutic value, the physical healing attributes, and the emotional uplift that comes when we pray to our heavenly Father in our heavenly language. I am delighted that he is writing a book so that others can share in the teaching and ministry of this man. As you read it, may you catch the spirit of this man, and be totally convinced of the value of the Baptism of the Holy Spirit."

HAROLD DUNCAN
SENIOR PASTOR, CENTURY ASSEMBLY
LODI, CALIFORNIA

"Stanford Linzey enjoyed a special anointing of the Holy Spirit when he expounded on the Scriptures that described the work of the third person of the Trinity. God used him in unique ways to bring untold numbers of people into the reality of a baptism in the Holy Spirit. Stanford Linzey distinguished himself as a dedicated scholar of the Scriptures, even at a time when his church fellowship did not offer strong endorsement or encouragement for scholarship. His preparation in this way opened the door for the military chaplaincy where his life impacted thousands of service men and women. This volume of Stanford Linzey's messages on the work of the Holy Spirit in the life of the believer has the potential of changing lives today and is another example of someone who has gone to be with the Lord still speaking to us with eloquence."

ROBERT H. SPENCE
PRESIDENT, EVANGEL UNIVERSITY
ASSEMBLIES OF GOD

"Dr. Stanford E. Linzey, Jr., has written an outstanding resource for anyone interested in learning more about the Spirit-filled life. In a day when many opinions grow out of a variety of personal experiences, we all need a biblical theology of the Holy Spirit. This book will both inform and inspire anyone who reads it. I highly commend it to you."

DON MEYER, PH.D.
PRESIDENT, VALLEY FORGE CHRISTIAN COLLEGE
ASSEMBLIES OF GOD

"After reading this manuscript I have relived many experiences with Dr. Stan Linzey because I have had him conduct services in every church I have pastored in California. His delivery was captivating. His gift was unique. His instruction was simple. His exegesis was Biblical. His manner was gentle. His interpretation of difficult passages was brilliant. His life was wholly dedicated to God and to help people in their spiritual walk. This book is vital reading for every pastor of all denominations and for all believers who want a deeper walk with the Lord. God has given Dr. Linzey a truly divine revelation of the purpose, the use, the manifestation, and instruction for ministering this gift and to make it all purposeful, receivable and practical. Some years ago I suggested to Dr. Linzey that he include some experiences from his military background and specifically the Battle of Midway to show the grace and mercy of God in his life. He did, and it blessed people greatly and gave them an understanding that God is in control of our lives all the time and everywhere."

HARRIS E. LIDSTRAND, D.MIN.
PRESIDENT, COMMUNITY CHRISTIAN COLLEGE, REDLANDS, CALIFORNIA
PASTOR FOR OVER 50 YEARS IN SOUTHERN CALIFORNIA
ASSEMBLIES OF GOD

"*Baptism in the Spirit* is a Biblically-based, testimony-filled account of a life planted by God in a strategic area: the Armed Forces of the United States of America. Stanford E. Linzey, Jr. was the first Assemblies of God chaplain to serve in the Navy and the first to achieve the rank of Captain. Most important, he served his God with a passion and led many to Christ and to the baptism in the Holy Spirit. Baptism is his story and it is an exciting one. Every reader will understand that the Holy Spirit is alive and well (!) and that the Book of Acts continues to be written even today. Do you wish to be filled with the Spirit and used by God? This testimony will tell you how, will encourage you, and give you a Biblical foundation for receiving the Spirit. Only eternity will reveal just how many people were touched by this amazing life placed in God's hands."

DAVID G. CLARK
PROFESSOR EMERITUS OF NEW TESTAMENT AND GREEK
VANGUARD UNIVERSITY OF SOUTHERN CALIFORNIA

"Dr. Linzey took a class on preaching at Fuller Theological Seminary when he was working on his Doctor of Ministry degree. Dr. Lloyd Ogilvie, who was the instructor, said that Chaplain Stan Linzey was the only one in the class who read Scripture with power and authority. Chaplain Linzey preached to the common man. To the sailor he was frank, practical and pointed. In the church, he was outspoken and clear. He forcefully spoke against biblically incorrect doctrine. It was a blessing and an inspiration to hear him speak at Southern California College and at a local church, and watch what the Holy Spirit did during the altar time. This book captures the oratorical style that Chaplain Linzey used."

REV. DAVID C. CLEAVELAND
CHAIRMAN, DEPARTMENT OF CHRISTIAN MINISTRIES
AMERICAN INDIAN COLLEGE OF THE ASSEMBLIES OF GOD

"Written in a clear, understandable, engaging, easy-to-read, conversational style, *Baptism in the Spirit* artfully blends biblical teaching, theological thought, and historical evidence in defense of the baptism in the Holy Spirit. Chockfull of anecdotes and spiced with piquant pieces of humor drawn from several decades of extensive and fruitful ministry, it answers legitimate questions and debunks many common misconceptions about the experience and invites every believer in Christ to an encounter with the Spirit that is necessary, vital, and relevant. We are indebted to Chaplain Stanford Linzey for a rich and valuable treasure."

TREVOR GRIZZLE, PH.D.
PROFESSOR OF NEW TESTAMENT
SCHOOL OF THEOLOGY AND MISSIONS
ORAL ROBERTS UNIVERSITY

"Stanford E. Linzey's book on *Baptism in the Spirit* is a delight to read. His communication style leaves no stone unturned and no one guessing as to what he just said. Anyone who wants to truly 'Get It' needs to read what he says about Spirit baptism. Captain Linzey is both humorous in his directness, yet sincere in his approach."

DAN WOODING
ASSIST NEWS SERVICE
FORMER JOURNALIST, BRITISH BROADCASTING CORPORATION

"Stanford Linzey exuded a peace and confidence in his Savior. Because of his work in the Spirit as a Chaplain in the United States Navy, I believe that untold numbers of men and women have come to Jesus and continue to come as a result of the seeds he planted. I was struck by the simplicity and directness of his understanding of the Holy Spirit—no smoke and mirrors, just the facts as presented by the Holy Word of God. In this book he thrusts a heavily-weighted knife, cutting through all denominations that have prejudice, and reveals a true interpretation of the Word."

WADE STEVERSON, PRESIDENT
BUSINESS MEN'S FELLOWSHIP, INTERNATIONAL
ESCONDIDO, CALIFORNIA
SOUTHERN BAPTIST

Acknowledgement

We would like to convey our heartfelt gratitude to Susan Milne for transcribing the tapes of Stan's series of sermons on *Baptism in the Spirit* for this book. She made this work a priority in her life and expedited the process. We are also extremely grateful to Shirley R. Felt, Ph.D., who is a former Chairman of the Humanities Division of Vanguard University of Southern California, for proofreading and assisting us in the final revision of these sermons after we edited them for readability. We would like to thank Professor David C. Cleaveland, to whom we owe a debt of gratitude, for his feedback and input to assist us in bringing out the meaning of archaic language for modern readers.

And I cannot forget to mention Father Michael Pacella, III, who as a sailor served with Stan aboard the USS *Coral Sea* when Stan was his Chaplain; served with my son Jim, both as Army Chaplains; and served as my "pastor" in the aftermath of Stan's passing away, for previewing the manuscript and sharing his thoughts with us. Finally, to the many military chaplains, pastors, academics, and friends who reviewed this manuscript and shared their perspectives, or reminisced of our ministry to them or to their congregations, I remember you. Stan and I deeply appreciated the bond we shared with you and still do share in the Spirit.

Verna M. Linzey, D.D.
Escondido, California
May 2012

PREFACE

When Stan and I first met 72 years ago on February 11, 1940, in San Diego, California, he was a Southern Baptist and I was a Classical Pentecostal, steeped in the Pentecostal Movement. I lived with my mother and step-father, Alice M. Hall and Rev. Francis L. Doyle, at that time, and Stan often came to visit me at our home. When religion came up in conversation, I introduced Stan to the teaching on the baptism with the Holy Spirit. Eventually, Stan received the baptism with the Holy Spirit as he describes in this book.

We married on July 13, 1941. This was the beginning of a lifetime of ministry in evangelizing and teaching classes and conducting services on Navy ships. During this time about 5,000 sailors and civilians were saved, and about 20,000 received the baptism with the Holy Spirit, which Stan later defined as *the reception of the Holy Spirit with the attendant manifestation of speaking in tongues.*

Eventually, Stan went to college and seminary and became the first Assembly of God chaplain to serve in the regular Navy, and in 1973, the first to attain the rank of Captain. In the early years of our marriage, Stan and I studied in great depth how the baptism was taught and was received in the Bible. We knew that, as Stan explains in this book, the method by which the baptism was received in the New Testament was just as relevant today as it was then. So using the methods the Bible taught and modeled, we began to teach and pray for many thousands of people to receive it.

Stan Linzey made Biblical theology on the baptism in the Holy Spirit easy for average people to understand and receive, explaining it in terms with which they were familiar. He brought the message down to the lowest common denominator for all to understand. His manner of communication was refreshing and delightful to the vast majority who listened to him and appreciated his directness as taught in US Navy leadership schools. He was easily understood by all, which is a sign of outstanding communication and preaching skills. In relating to average people, he sometimes preferred slang over verbal eloquence to get the point across. Whereas his former books illustrate Stan's finesse in his excellent writing abilities, this book is comprised of transcripts of what he actually said. It illustrates his personality and how he related with people through speaking. Reading this book will make you feel you are listening to him speak directly to you.

We have set forth in this book, *Baptism in the Spirit,* Stan's series of messages on the baptism which he preached for several decades. We have taken taped messages from 1973, which were delivered by Stan before a live audience, and transcribe and edit them for a reading audience. What you are about to read are the sermons which built Stan's reputation, with all the insight he gleaned through the years, which have impacted thousands of people's lives over the course of most of our evangelistic ministry.

Stan's main contribution to the Church and to the world has been his ministry and teaching on the baptism in the Holy Spirit. In his later years, he would change the thrust of his speaking and writing to what God did in servicemen's personal lives leading up to and following the Battle of Midway in World War II.

The legacy of Stan's life was the impact he made with his teaching and ministry on the baptism with the Holy Spirit, and the culmination of his influence was reflected in participating on

President George W. Bush's stage on August 28, 2005. Standing behind the Seal of the President of the United States of America at Coronado Naval Air Station on North Island in San Diego, Stan delivered the invocation before President Bush spoke for the 60th Anniversary of the Japanese Surrender in World War II.

I would like to thank Stan for making this work easily accomplished. His clarity of thought and speech has made this an enriching and unencumbered task, for his eloquence has given us much to work with in the editing process. Stan's series of presentations on the baptism in the Holy Spirit are laid out in a very straightforward manner. We believe that the reader will be inspired by being able to connect with Stanford E. Linzey, Jr., in *Baptism in the Spirit*.

May this book change your life and impart Scriptural understanding and practical considerations to free you to begin praying in the Spirit, for "the promise is unto you and, to your children, and to all who are afar off . . . " (Acts 2:39). May God richly bless the study of His Word through Stanford E. Linzey, Jr., and, through this book, continue to lead many more thousands of people into the Pentecostal experience of the baptism in the Holy Spirit with its accompanying manifestations and gifts.

Verna M. Linzey, D.D.
Escondido, California
May 2012

FOREWORD

Chaplain Stanford Linzey's sermons on the Holy Spirit have been used by God to bring thousands into the Pentecostal experience with its initial evidence of speaking in tongues. This book compiles a sequence of sermons that continues to bring faith and obedience to many more.

My biblical theology, *What the Bible Says about the Holy Spirit,* is used as a textbook in many languages. However, it does not attempt to answer all the questions that are asked by Baptists and other non-Pentecostal believers and by unbelievers as well. Chaplain Linzey not only answers them biblically, but illustrates them from his many experiences as a navy chaplain, as a pastor, and as an evangelist who traveled the world. He also challenges people to believe and act. The fact that many who attend our Assemblies of God or other Pentecostal churches have not yet been baptized in the Holy Spirit, and many who have been baptized no longer speak or pray in tongues, is another reason these sermons are needed. Whether you agree with everything Stanford says or not, that much cannot be denied.

I have read these sermons and recommend them as encouragement for all who have questions about the baptism in the Holy Spirit. Stan Linzey answers just about every possible question by explaining Bible passages and by illustrating with many interesting and encouraging stories. I especially appreciate his emphasis on the fact that "tarrying" is not needed.

My early seeking was like his early seeking. But when I said in prayer, "If there is a freedom in speaking in tongues, I want it," suddenly I began speaking in tongues loudly and freely. It was easier to pray in tongues than to pray in English.

The mother of one of our missionaries told me not to let a day go by without speaking in or praying in tongues. I should have known that there was no need for tarrying.

In 1885, my grandmother got up to speak to a group of Baptist women in a suburb of Erie, Pennsylvania. Suddenly, she began to speak in a language she had never learned. Then she gave an interpretation that was all Scripture and fitted together to form a message. When her husband, Elmer Fisher, a Baptist pastor, took her to the Azusa Street mission in Los Angeles, and she sensed what was going on, she said, "I already have this." They said, "You couldn't have, you are a Baptist." She didn't argue. She knelt and began to pray in tongues. People were already coming from all over the world, and a man from Denmark said she was speaking in Danish. They got my mother, then 11 years old, down to be sanctified, but in less than ten minutes she was speaking in tongues, this time in French. It was truly like the Day of Pentecost.

My prayer is that every hungry person who reads Stan Linzey's sermons will be baptized, speak in tongues, and then walk in the Spirit in obedience to God's Word.

Stanley Monroe Horton, Th.D.
May 2012

DEDICATION

Stan, this book is dedicated to your legacy. Your experience in the baptism in the Holy Spirit 71 years ago has had a ripple effect, changing the world. May this book continue to preach the message so long as Jesus tarries.

In loving memory,

Verna M. Linzey, D.D.
Escondido, California
May 2012

TABLE OF CONTENTS

INTRODUCTION

We're happy with what God is doing. And I tell you, in this day and time, when anybody receives the baptism with the Holy Spirit, it's a wonderful thing. Our emphasis is going to be concerning the baptism with the Holy Spirit.

We want you to pray. Let's have prayer and shout the glory a little bit before we start. It takes prayer and worship to have the Spirit move in our lives. God is no respecter of people. If God can do it at one place, God can do it in another place. And you'll say a good "Amen" to that.

In this day and time we need the baptism in the Holy Spirit just to make us the kind of people we ought to be. Do you hear me? It takes all of God we can get to be the kind of people we ought to be today. Now I don't want you to miss a chapter. In each chapter, I'll be sharing on the doctrine of the baptism in the Holy Spirit. By the time I've finished, I will have discussed, entirely, from a doctrinal viewpoint, the main issues concerning the baptism in the Holy Spirit.

In chapter one, we'll be discussing Prophesy and Doctrine, using as our text Joel 2 and the Gospels.

In chapter two, we'll be discussing the Day of Pentecost. Here we will examine Acts 2.

In chapter three, we'll be discussing Cornelius the Roman officer and his household in Acts 10.

In chapter four, we offer another doctrinal study dealing with Acts 19 and the Ephesian Jews. Now these are all different, and there's a textual situation I want you to be sure to get in this.

And in chapter five, we'll be discussing Acts chapter 8. We'll be discussing the revival in Samaria, and there is an exegetical part of the text. I do want to bring that to your attention because you'll need it. You should understand it. I would to God that more were reading it. But what I have to tell you would be helpful not only to yourself, but also in helping you tell somebody else about it. We need to tell other people what it's all about, and that's what I'm trying to help you do in this series of messages.

Acts 2, 10, 19, and 8 are the four main Scriptures in Acts dealing with the baptism. So don't miss a segment on it at all. Every message will have something you need to know and have needed to know for a long time. I've been through a Baptist college, two Baptist seminaries, and the Harvard Divinity School. So we've had all the questions asked that can be asked, nearly, and we've come through with a pretty good situation here. What I'm doing is laying it out so people can know what they should believe, and have a reason of the hope that is within them. So don't miss a chapter, will you?

In chapter six, I'll be sharing on the subject, "Why Speak with Tongues?" from I Corinthians 14. This will be highly informative, and I assure you it's material that some of you have never heard in your life. This is not just scriptural. But also, I'll be telling you what the medical profession is saying about it—those who know. It's a very good thing to know and have in your own armory when you're speaking about these things. Now this is not as simple as you think. You know, we Pentecostal people are an odd lot sometimes. Oh, we're good people. But I mean we do things in a funny way. We read the Scriptures in a hurry, and we generally think, "Whatever the most obvious answer is, that's right!" But that's not generally true. The most obvious thing we think we see in the Scriptures generally isn't correct. Generally, the thing you have to dig out is what's correct. So, I'm going to be sharing on the subject, "Why Speak with Tongues?" Don't miss this. I'll have a lot of things for you to consider, along with what others and psychotherapists are saying about this situation. How can you tell if it's gibberish or tongues? This will be discussed. This will be worth your time to hear. Then I will also be telling you about the occasion when I preached in the Pentagon in Washington, D.C. on the baptism in the Holy Spirit, about the people who received the Holy Spirit and what they are doing. It is a thrilling story. We had a good time. I'll tell you for sure. It'll be a story you'll never forget. Don't miss this.

Then in chapter seven, our final message in this series, I will be sharing on the subject "After Tongues, What?" from Galatians 5. Now you won't want to miss this. You'll need this after we've finished the doctrine of tongues. I have some thrilling things I want to tell you about that. So plan to read it. We're going to tell you what you ought to be doing since you've got the baptism in the Holy Spirit and giving you some real flesh and blood illustrations of how it works. So keep those things in mind and plan to be with us through this series. You'll need this to round out the course.

By the time we have finished this series of messages, you will have had a good course dealing with the baptism in the Holy Spirit as is brought out in Acts chapters 2, 8, 10, and 19. So take notes. It's a good thing to do. And quite frankly, I don't know anybody else that's laying it out in quite this fashion. But like I say, we've had to work our way through the Baptist colleges and seminaries with it. When you deal with the Baptists, you have to read the Word. And we appreciate them for that.

In Pentecost, we hear everything in the world. Every preacher comes home and has got something to tell you, and it does get confusing at times.

In this book we're going to be answering the questions that many of you have on your mind and nobody ever answers. Do you ever have questions that nobody ever answers? Or do you go to hear preaching and they always preach on something you don't need to know? But there are generally some questions you have on your mind that no one ever talks about. During this course of study we should answer all your questions concerning this subject, "The Baptism in the Holy Spirit."

One question is, "When a person speaks in tongues, does the Holy Spirit speak through that person?" No, don't look for the obvious answer. It may not be true. We'll be discussing that and answering that question.

Another question is, "When a person is seeking the baptism in the Holy Spirit, can that person get a wrong experience? Can I get the wrong thing?" Don't look for the obvious. We'll be discussing that.

It is sometimes asked, "Is holiness a criterion to receive the baptism in the Holy Spirit?" A concomitant question will be, "How holy do you have to be?" And then we're going to discuss, "Whose standard are we going by?" It's a pretty good subject, really. And it's a pretty good question. Don't miss this because these are things you need to know, and we will be discussing them.

Now I've got one thing I want to say: don't get too serious. If you get too serious, we can't do much. Let's lighten the load. What do you say? Let's lighten the load a little bit. Let's enjoy our religion. What do you say? I was in one place, and I got to talking like this, and when church was over, we had a good time. One party said, "You sure made going to church enjoyable." Well, that's what it ought to be. You ought to enjoy going to church! And so we hope to make it enjoyable for you.

It seems like I've said enough about that. So you keep these issues in mind. We'll be reminding you of these from chapter to chapter.

Now these messages are shared on my own time. Can you imagine a Navy man taking annual leave just to share? That's what I've done, and that's our business here. Just to share with you people. Please don't miss one chapter. You have time to do everything you want to do anyway.

This series of messages will be entirely on the baptism in the Holy Spirit. I say this because sometimes we have denominational friends who will say, "That's all you people talk about." Well that is going to be all we talk about in this series of messages. Now we know some other things. We've read a couple of books in our life. We know a few other things, too. But that's not the emphasis. The emphasis here is on the Holy Spirit. And so we're narrowing down to this for this particular series.

Now everybody can receive the baptism in the Holy Spirit. Everybody! I don't care who you are, or where you come from. I don't hold out any gimmicks. I don't hold out any shortcuts. But I do hold out the Word of God, and I believe in the Bible. Can you say a good "Amen"? And I will have Scriptures to offer for the things I have to say. In these chapters, I will show you how to receive the Holy Spirit. "And you mean you're going to tell us how?" That's right! I'm going to tell you how. Nobody else will, so I've decided to do it. How about that? You can't beat that, can you? And so I think that's pretty brave, and I'm kind of happy with that. I'm going to show you how to cooperate with the Lord in receiving. Bear in mind, I do not give the Holy Spirit. Our Lord Jesus Christ is He who baptizes with the Holy Spirit. You can say "Amen" to that. However, as a servant of Jesus Christ, I do teach on the Holy Spirit. Now that's Scriptural. We'll be discussing this in chapters to come. I can show you some ways to cooperate, and how to yield, and we certainly need teaching along these lines.

To some of you, my method may seem novel. But God has shown me some things for you. All you have to do is be attentive and cooperative. Pastors have brought me to their churches for the good of the people. Now some of my methods may shatter you. But if up to this time you have not received the baptism in the Holy Spirit, anything would be better than what you're doing. That just makes good sense, doesn't it! So if what you have been doing hasn't been working, you might as well try what I'm going to tell you. One more thing can't hurt anyway. Over twenty thousand people took my suggestions and received the baptism in the Holy Spirit. So you want to keep that in mind.

I'm bringing you a message of fact and faith. I'm going to present the facts and I hope you have the faith to receive them. I'm going to be giving instructions from chapter to chapter on receiving the Holy Spirit. Now I'm happy to be sharing. Your church may have had others in the charismatic line share. That's fine. That's great. Others may have said different things. And that's quite all right. What I'm going to be telling you is what God has shown me. In your mind, don't compare me with somebody else. That's not the way to do. Rather, take what I've got to say and keep it in context. And let's see what God has for you. Sometimes my mannerisms are rather brusque or crude. If for any reason you think I am crude or rude, or uncouth, to help you get along with it and to bear with me, just say to yourself, "He's in the Navy, and he can't help it."

I do not believe in tarrying to receive the Holy Spirit. I don't believe it's a New Testament term at all. We'll be telling you more about this. So, when I get into this, some of you will think that what I have to present seems to be rather mechanical. Well, it might to start out. But I would say that that's where your faith comes in. If you're going to depend upon feeling, then you don't need faith, do you! But you don't go by feelings; you go by faith in God's Word and what it says. I heard somebody say one time, "Yes, but doesn't that give a rather minimal experience?" Of course, my answer to that is, "Yes, but it's more than you had." In other words, take what God gives you and work from there. Sure! And again, in receiving the baptism in the Holy Spirit, for so long a time we've held it up as a goal to be attained. That's wrong. Receiving the baptism in the Holy Spirit—that's a door you enter through and begin something. It's only the beginning. Then God's got more for you after that. But you do need to get past the beginning. And all we're trying to do is get you through the door and get you started on the way. Hallelujah! Okay, so I guess that takes care of that.

Incidentally, sometimes I use poor grammar to get a point across. Again, it's intentional, because you can just seem to get an emphasis with poor grammar that you can't get with good grammar. I don't know why that is, but it is.

Stanford E. Linzey, Jr.
Anchorage, Alaska
1973

1

PROPHESY AND DOCTRINE
OLD TESTAMENT AND GOSPELS

Old Testament

I suppose we can start by saying that in Old Testament times, it appears that God was a respecter of people. I say that because in the Old Testament dispensation, God did not give the Holy Spirit to everybody. In fact, He gave the Holy Spirit only to people in authority: for example, the priests, the kings, the prophets, or the various redeemers who came along from time to time like Samson and Gideon. The Spirit came on Gideon; he blew a trumpet and went to war. Samson was a man of superhuman strength. The Holy Spirit came upon these people betimes, it says. That means once in a while, to perform a task that God had for them to perform. He did not come to indwell their hearts as we know Him today.

Not only that, the Holy Spirit did not come upon women. You women ought to be glad you live in a New Testament dispensation. In the Old Testament days, women were not even counted in the number. They were chattel, property. However, there are always exceptions to the rule. And on one occasion God blessed Deborah, a prophetess, who was mightily used of God. But if you read the story carefully, God used her on that occasion because a man would not do what God wanted him to do. Men, I'm going to tell you something, and I've got news for you. If God wants you to do something, you'd better to do it, because if you don't, He'll raise up a woman to do it, and she'll get the job done. You can't beat a woman who's got her mind made up to do something. I'll tell you for sure. And don't think, men, that He can't get along without you. He can. He will. And so God used Deborah on this occasion.

The Prophet Joel

Now the prophet Joel came some 800 years prior to the time of Jesus Christ. The Spirit of prophecy came upon him, and he said in Joel 2:28-29, "And it shall come to pass afterward, that I will pour out my Spirit upon all flesh; and your sons and your daughters shall prophesy, your old men shall dream dreams, your young men shall see visions; And also upon the servants and upon the handmaidens in those days will I pour out my Spirit." Joel is saying that the time will come when God will give his Spirit to everybody regardless of rank or station in life, or regardless of whether they are male or female. It won't make any difference. God will give the Holy Spirit to everybody.

Gospels

We're going to skip the 800 years rather rapidly and move over into the New Testament era. And as we do so, we read in Matthew 3. John the Baptist, the forerunner of Jesus Christ, has come on the scene preaching a baptism of repentance. Now this is water baptism. Baptism is not a new thing. The Jews had baptisms, washings, ablution,[1] and all of this. So this was not a new thing. John simply was the last of the great prophets and made something out of it in his time. Boy he was having success because it appears that the whole countryside was turning out to hear John preach and many were repenting of their sins and being baptized in Jordan. Then John makes this statement in Matthew 3:11, "I indeed baptize you with water unto repentance: but He that cometh after me is mightier than I, whose shoes I am not worthy to bear: He shall baptize you with the Holy Spirit and with fire."

Three Baptisms

Now for the first time in the Bible, and certainly the first time in the New Testament, we have the baptism with the Holy Spirit mentioned here. This is meaningful. This is not a play on words. If you go to the Greek text, that's exactly what it says. John is baptizing in water; Jesus will baptize with the Holy Spirit. All of a sudden, two baptisms are noted. One is water baptism, one is Spirit baptism. In water baptism, a man is the agent and the water is the element, and a person is baptized in water. In Spirit baptism, Jesus Christ is the agent and the Holy Spirit is the element, and a person is baptized into the Holy Spirit.

There is one other significant baptism I'll mention, though we're not concerned with it. That is the baptism into the body of Christ, in which the Holy Spirit is the agent, the body of Christ is the element, and the individual is baptized into the body of Christ. Every man or woman, boy or girl, who is saved, has been baptized by the Holy Spirit into the body of Christ. Let's make no mistake about that. If you're saved, you're in the body of Christ. The Holy Spirit put you in the body of Christ. You have been baptized in the body of Christ. If you have not been baptized in water you should be. You ought to follow the Lord in water baptism. And if you have not received the baptism of the Holy Spirit, you can.

The Comforter

Now, we move on into the Gospel according to John, chapter 14. Jesus Christ followed John the Baptist and grew to manhood. Then He had a ministry perhaps of some two-and-a-half or three years. Jesus had told His people, "I will never leave you nor forsake you" (Heb. 13:5). However, the time is coming in which He would be betrayed, be crucified, die and be buried, and then rise from the dead. But the problem is, how is He going to keep the promise, "I will never leave you nor forsake you?" Well He told us in John 14. And we read it in verses 16-18. Jesus said, "I will pray the Father, and He shall give you another Comforter, that He may abide with you forever; Even the Spirit of truth; whom the world cannot receive, because it seeth Him not, neither knoweth Him; but ye know Him, for He dwelleth with you, and shall be in you. I will not leave you comfortless." All right, here we have it. He's going to give them the Comforter. He's going to give them the Holy Spirit who will do the same thing that Jesus Christ had done and will continue to be with the disciples. He will be with them in the person of the Holy Spirit. Hallelujah!

Every Believer Receives the Holy Spirit

Now let's go back to John 14:17 and let me give you a little exegesis on the text. You need this. I have heard well-meaning Pentecostals, particularly if they're trying to tell a good Baptist about the Holy Spirit, use verse 17 to tell the Baptist about the Holy Spirit, and say, "He is with you now, but He'll be in you when you receive the baptism." And they triumphantly think they've proved the point. How wrong can you be? That's not true at all. Anybody who knows the Bible knows that every believer already has the Holy Spirit. For Paul said in Romans 8:9, "If any man have not the Spirit of Christ, he is none of His." Every believer has the Holy Spirit. Don't tell a good Baptist he hasn't got the Holy Spirit. He's as saved as you are, if he's saved. And don't tell this to a Presbyterian, or a Methodist or a Catholic or anybody else. If they love Jesus Christ and have embraced the Gospel, they have received the Holy Spirit. Don't make any mistake on that. They're brothers and sisters in Christ.

Well, what does this mean then? That's what I'm going to tell you, so you will understand. We don't read very critically, do we? We don't read very carefully, do we? Now at the time Jesus said this, the Holy Spirit had not yet been given because Jesus had not yet been glorified. When He said "He's with you," the Holy Spirit was with them in the person of Jesus Christ. He was with them in the person of Christ. Jesus said, "It is expedient for you that I go away: for if I go not away, the Comforter will not come unto you; but if I depart, I will send Him unto you" (John 16:7). In other words, Christ had to depart this earth so that the Holy Spirit might be given. Then we can say that the Holy Spirit was captive to the body of Jesus while Jesus was here in the flesh. "For in Him dwelleth all the fullness of the Godhead bodily" (Col. 2:9). It took the death of Jesus Christ to release the Spirit to the world! Now this makes sense. And this is doctrinally true, and keeps the Scriptures consummate with themselves. So the Holy Spirit was with them in the person of Jesus. Therefore He says He is with you, but He shall be in you when Jesus goes away. Then He's going to come into your heart and live within your heart. That's the meaning of the text here. So don't ever tell another good Baptist that he doesn't have the Holy Spirit, because if he knows the Bible, he'll pin your ears to the wall with the Scriptures.

Christ's Final Command

Jesus then was crucified, dead and buried, and risen again. After the resurrection, He was on the earth some forty days before the ascension took place. And He met with His disciples several times. Now we go back over into the book of Luke. And here in Chapter 24 of Luke, we have the last command given. I'm amazed at how many Christians think that the last command of Jesus was to go into the world and preach the gospel to every creature. That was not the last command. That was the next-to-the-last command. The last command is given here in Luke 24:49-53, "And behold, I send the promise of my Father upon you; but tarry ye in the city of Jerusalem, until ye be endued[2] with power from on high. And He led them out as far as to Bethany, and He lifted up His hands, and blessed them. And it came to pass, while He blessed them, He was parted from them, and carried up into heaven. And they worshipped Him, and returned to Jerusalem with great joy, and were continually in the temple praising and blessing God."

I can just hear some old-time Pentecostal say, "Uh-huh! It did say 'tarry!'" Well sure it did. But, of course, again, I've got to ask you the question, "How do you read?" Some of us don't read very critically, do we! We don't know really what we are reading. Again, I have to tell you that the word "tarry" is really not a holy word. All it means is *wait*. It's a King James word. And another thing, this is pre-Pentecost. The Holy Spirit had not yet been given because

Christ had not yet been glorified. And, again, I have to tell you this. At the time Jesus said it, the gift of the Holy Spirit had not been given. You know, there's one thing about it. If somebody's going to give you a gift, you pretty well have to wait 'til he gives it, don't you! You're not going to get it before he gives it, unless you steal it or drag it out of him somehow. Of course, you're not going to drag this out of Jesus in any way.

But, on the other hand, after one gives a gift, you might wonder why you're still tarrying³. Right? That doesn't make too much sense either, does it! Supposing I meet the gunner down there and I say:

"Hey gunner, I'll meet you on the street tomorrow afternoon. Tomorrow, we'll go down and have a cup of coffee, okay?"

"Okay."

"Now, whoever gets there first waits on the other fellow."

"Okay, fine."

And so, three o'clock is the appointment. And so, at three o'clock we go down to one of the cafes and meet over coffee. And supposing I say to myself, "Well, you know, gunner probably won't be on time anyway. I'll get there about 3:15."

And Gunner says to himself, "Chaplain might be early; I'll get there at 2:45." So he gets there at 2:45 and he waits.

And I come dragging in at 3:15. And I say, "I sure appreciate you waiting, gunny. You know how it is. I got held up a little bit, and I'm glad you waited for me. Now, I'm going to wait for you a while."

He'd probably say, "Well, what do you mean?"

And suppose I replied, "Well you were kind enough to wait for me, so I'm going to wait for you."

"But I'm already here," Gunny says.

"I know it." He'd probably think that the chaplain's a pretty good guy, but he's just been at sea too long, you know.

But isn't that the way we behave sometimes with regard to the Holy Spirit? The Holy Spirit's been given and we're still tarrying. We don't know why. Somebody said "Do it," and it sounded really good, so we've been doing it. We're a good bunch of people. We do what people tell us to do. If you tell them to tarry, they tarry. If you tell them to get it, they get it. So we're going to be telling you to get it! Hallelujah! You've been tarrying long enough, and you don't even know why you've been doing it. But the disciples were there, waiting until the Holy Spirit would be given.

The Book of Luke-Acts

Now let's go on over to the first chapter of the book of Acts. We're covering a lot of ground here, aren't we! But then we want to do it because we want to get the groundwork set. I told my wife, "I ought to bring a bunch of certificates along, and give everybody that makes every lesson a certificate when it's over with, having completed the course." One of the old-timers said, "This is the finest course I've ever had on the baptism of the Holy Spirit." That made me feel pretty good.

The disciple Luke wrote the book of Luke. He also wrote the book of Acts. Now when Luke and Acts came out, originally it came out as a two-part, one-volume work, called the Book of Luke-Acts. Anybody who reads will know that in a sequel volume, generally there's a little overlap from the last few pages of the first volume and the first few pages of the second volume. And we have that here. We just read Luke 24 about tarrying in Jerusalem. Now we have the same thought here in Acts 1:4-5. Luke said, speaking of Jesus, "And, being assembled together with them, commanded them that they should not depart from Jerusalem, but wait for the promise of the Father, which, saith He, you have heard of Me. For John truly baptized with water; but ye shall be baptized with the Holy Spirit not many days hence."

The Term "Baptism in the Holy Spirit"

Now this is beautiful. I wish every one of you were Baptist because I'd really love to give this to you straight. I'm going to do it anyway. This is good medicine for Baptists, because it makes them squirm. And I was born and reared a southern Baptist. It says, "John truly baptized with water, but ye shall be baptized with the Holy Spirit not many days hence" (Acts 1:5). Now that's not a play on terms. That's what Jesus' words said.

When you get to the second chapter of Acts and see what took place, you would have to come to the conclusion, if you have any reasoning powers at all, that whatever took place there, with all the attending phenomena, would be called the baptism with the Holy Spirit. That's just sensible. "Ye shall be baptized with the Holy Spirit not many days hence" (Acts 1:5). In the second chapter of Acts it happens. So you might write down Matthew 3:11, and Acts 1:5, because I will be hitting upon them from time to time. Even the Baptist agrees that whatever's going to happen has to be called the baptism in the Holy Spirit. Don't forget these points because I'll be coming back to them.

The Purpose for Receiving the Baptism with the Holy Spirit

Now Acts 1:8 tells us the main purpose for receiving the baptism of the Holy Spirit. The baptism with the Holy Spirit is not given to you to make you shout, nor to make you feel good, nor to make you run around the church. Now let me say right quickly that your church belongs to you. You're paying the bills with your tithes and offerings. If you want to run around it, that's all right. I've got nothing against that. You understand that, don't you! And I enjoy seeing people do gymnastics once in a while myself. That's good exercise, if nothing else. And I've got nothing against all of that. I was somewhere preaching one time. I was on a high platform. And a little fellow got up there. I don't know how he got up there, but he did, along with another boy. He got so filled with joy and happiness. He began going around and around, and he fell off to the deck below, which was concrete, right on his head. Now by all rights that should have broken his neck. But it didn't. He got up and kept shouting the glory. I think that's marvelous. But he was having a good time. You know what I heard about another person? I heard that a guy got up on the front row of pews and ran down the pews across the backs. And he got up, and he come up the other side. Now, you know, that's dangerous. If he had missed one, he'd break his neck. No doubt!

Well, now, that's not power. That's energy. But if people want to do it, I have nothing against it. I'll tell you one thing, friend. If you belong to a good Pentecostal church, stay in it. It's worth your money to see the show once in a while. You never know what's going to happen. There's nothing like human nature after all is said and done. These shows downtown can't compare with some of the things we do. I'll tell you for sure. And it's all free. They do it for nothing, you know! And it's really a good deal. I'll tell you!

But Acts 1:8 says that you receive power to persuade men and women concerning Jesus Christ. You're supposed to be able to win somebody to the Lord. How often our people say, "Well, I just can't do it. The Lord hasn't called me." Wait a minute! You've got it all backward. Every Christian is called to be a witness. Every Christian! I don't care how poor of a Christian you are.

I'm a disciple of Trueblood. He was a Quaker from Earlham College. If you want to read something good, read Elton Trueblood. He wrote a book called *The Company of the Committed*. This is one of the finest I've ever read. He says that there's no such thing as a non-witnessing Christian. It's a contradiction in terms. Some of you people haven't been doing any witnessing. What's the matter with you? And, particularly, if you've received the baptism of the Holy Ghost and you haven't been witnessing for Jesus Christ, what's the matter with you? Something's wrong with you! You bet there's something wrong with you!

The trouble is we spend our time doing wrong things so much of the time, things we ought not to be doing sometimes, when we ought to be witnessing for Jesus Christ. I'll tell you what! If you get prayed up and filled with the Holy Ghost and begin doing something for Jesus Christ, and get filled with the power of God, and get filled with the love of God, and begin to see men and women come to Christ, He'll keep you living straight and doing right! There's a few of them. Hallelujah!

From Prairie Bible Institute in Three Hills, Alberta, Canada, Dr. L.E. Maxwell, was one of the finest—a Baptist, if you please. He met a party he had known quite a while. He said to them, "How are you doing?

And the party said, "Well, I'm serving God the best I can in my small weak way."

Dr. Maxwell boomed back, "You ought not have any weak ways."

The Upper Room

We make excuses too often. Be filled with the Spirit and power for service. Acts 1:15 tells us that on the Day of Pentecost there were about 120 people present who received the baptism with the Holy Spirit. Now we have some people in the land today, namely the Church of Christ people who are good about this. They can quote you Scripture by the yard, but they don't always know what it means. They haven't got it hooked up right! They're pretty good people. But if you teach them to read, they would know something. They're really good people. But when they read the Scriptures, they say that only the twelve were there. I don't know how in the world they get that out of the Scriptures, because they're wrong on three counts.

In the first place, it says there were about 120. In the second place, they say there were 12 disciples there; but there were only 11 disciples since Judas wasn't there. So they missed it on that one. And so that can't be solved. And I don't know how you get the 12 unless you divide 120 by 10. And I don't know any reach for doing that. So they missed it all the way around.

Now don't feel bad. Some of you are cringing. "He's talking about people." I talk about all of them! I even talk against the

Assemblies once in a while! I'm free to talk about anybody I want to talk about! No malice in my heart! I love them all. Hallelujah! And even some of my people think I'm all right. But then, that's all right.

But the point is, I spoke on this at Bethel Church in San Jose, California. Dr. Leland Keys was the pastor at the time. And I made this same statement. When I talk about churches, people become worried. Don't worry! You worry too much! That'll take the joy out of your religion, so don't worry! I made that statement, but, oh, what a meeting we had! It's a huge church. And when they filled the prayer room, they filled the prayer room entirely with people wanting the baptism. In fact, there were so many I could not even give instructions. I said, "People raise your hands, start worshiping God. He'll fill some of you before I even lay my hands on you." And He did. In about 30 minutes, 40 or 50 people received a wonderful infilling of the Holy Spirit. At one point, a little gray-haired man came up to me with his wife, and said, "Chaplain, would you lay hands on us to receive the Holy Spirit?" I said, "Yes, sir." I laid hands on the little man and his wife and they received a wonderful infilling. Friends in the church told us the next Wednesday that he and his wife were Church of Christ believers. They took 25 minutes out of Dr. Keys' time to tell the Assemblies of God people how good it was. Hallelujah! Well, we just showed them how to read. So you've got to do that. Love them all. Preach to them all. Help them all. Pray with them all. That's what we do. And because of it, we've seen all kinds of denominational people come to Jesus. We love them all.

2

THE DAY OF PENTECOST
ACTS 2

Now we finally get to the second chapter of Acts. "And when the day of Pentecost was fully come, they were all with one accord in one place. And suddenly there came a sound from heaven as of a rushing mighty wind, and it filled all the house where they were sitting. And there appeared unto them cloven tongues like as of fire, and it sat upon each of them. And they were all filled with the Holy Spirit, and began to speak with other tongues, as the Spirit gave them utterance" (Acts 2:1-4).

Jesus said in Acts 1:5, "Ye shall be baptized with the Holy Spirit not many days hence." Here it is ten days from then. The Day of Pentecost has come. This is the day God has chosen. They are filled with the Holy Spirit. They are baptized in the Holy Spirit. This is a New Testament phenomenon, if you please.

Bear in mind, their much praying did not bring the Holy Spirit. The Holy Spirit was coming anyway at Pentecost. We need to understand that. Your much praying and your much tarrying will not bring the baptism to you. Not at all! This is all God's doing. I believe in the sovereignty of God. Hallelujah! But it was their good fortune to be there and to receive when the Holy Spirit was given. So the disciples waited ten days, not knowing what was going to happen. And when the Holy Spirit came, they all spoke with tongues as the Holy Spirit gave utterance. Fourteen or fifteen languages or more were spoken on this occasion. Now these were languages that were understood in the world at that time—known languages, if you please. We hear the people in the crowd saying later on how they heard in their own tongue from where they were born. There were about two million Jews in Jerusalem at this time, attending the feast of Pentecost. God knows when to throw a meeting, doesn't he! The feast comes when He's got the people there. That's when He sends the Holy Spirit. And they are filled.

Now there's one thing about this. The people who received the baptism are Galilean Jews. This is the dumb type of Jew. And there aren't many dumb Jews, believe me. By dumb, I mean these are not the elite Jews. And these are the ones doing the speaking in tongues. And it certainly raises questions.

Accusation of Drunkenness

Now you always have wise guys in every age and dispensation. And so they had a wise guy back then. I suppose he represented some people, because when they couldn't understand how it was happening, this fellow said, "These people are all drunk." Now that's an amazing conclusion to come to, isn't it! Here's somebody talking a foreign language he's never heard, and he says, "He's drunk." Well, the only thing you can draw from that kind of reasoning is, if getting drunk will help you learn a language, let's all get drunk! Now, don't go out and do like one party did. I said that at one place, and one party went out and said, "The chaplain said we all ought to go get drunk!" No, I didn't say we ought to get drunk. I'm saying that that's the kind of reasoning that would come from this sort of speech. Even if you took the Bible as mere literature, this is an interesting phenomenon. If you notice what happens in the Scriptures, a person's actions often give a reason to preach; someone always has to do something which needs to be explained or answered by someone else preaching a sermon. First somebody does something; then a guy gets up and preaches. That's what happened here. This fellow comes along and says, "They're all drunk," and that gives Peter a reason to preach. That's beautiful, isn't it! Sure it is. Peter couldn't have preached if this guy hadn't done that. So he did it.

Peter's Pentecostal Sermon

And so, here's Peter. Here's the fellow who denied the Christ so miserably! I'm going to tell you, if he can get it, you can get it. He's the one that said, "I don't know him!" Here he is. He's the guy that rises up. When the wise guy said, "They're drunk," ol' Peter rose up and said in verse 15-16, "These are not drunken, as ye suppose, seeing it is but the third hour of the day. But this is that which was spoken by the prophet Joel." And then he quotes Joel's prophecy verbatim. What Joel had said 800 years ago has finally come to pass. This is it! And for your information, there were both men and women in the group. Mary, the mother of Jesus was there. It wasn't just the 12, if you please. She was counted in the number. And, of course, after saying all of this, the wise guy just gave Peter the Apostle a reason to preach. So he went ahead and preached Christ to them. And the result was that some three thousand were saved that day and baptized in water. This was the Day of Pentecost, the beginning, the birth day of the New Testament church in any theologian's notebook.

We're going to stop with this passage right here. We will take up studying the Scriptures in the next chapter. And believe me, friends, it does get interesting.

Practical Factors

Now I want to get on over into some practical factors that will help you in receiving the Holy Spirit. These are very practical to be sure. And those of you who haven't received, I want you to hear this, because it'll help you overcome some things.

Old Time Pentecostal Meetings

I'm not too old. But I can remember being in some of the old time Pentecostal meetings. Brother, I mean, the meetings went all night, nearly. Do you remember some of those meetings? I mean, they preached half the night. And then if they got somebody needing a baptism, they'd get the victim down. I'm going to tell you, he thought he was a victim, because when they got him down there they wouldn't let him go. They were going to make him stay there 'til he got it. Can you remember some of those old days? Boy, it was great. I mean, there would be one bunch of people together, and they'd pound it in his back. Or they'd massage it in. Somebody on one side would say, "Let go, brother." And he didn't know what to let go of. And somebody on the opposite side would say, "Hold on, brother." And he didn't know what to hold on to. It was confusing signals, to be sure. And, generally, the person who wanted to do the closest personal work usually ate garlic and onions before he got there and blew it right in the victim's face. Those were good old days, I'll tell you for sure.

And then they do everything in order to make people comfortable, too, you know. I remember one time, my oldest son was a lad. He was seeking the baptism. And the old ladies of the church were trying to help the lad. And, you know, they were good ladies. So they got a pillow for the lad to lay his head on. That was nice. And so we were trying to help the lad get the baptism. You know how it goes. You pray 'til you're just about worn out, and you quit. Somebody else carries it on. You get a second wind, and you start it again. And so the time came that the lad got quiet.

Then we went home. He didn't get the baptism that night, but he did later. But one time, later on, he said, "Dad, you remember when I was tarrying for the baptism in the tavern?"

I replied, "Yeah."

He said, "You remember that time it got real quiet?"

I said, "Yeah."

He said, "You know what happened?"

"What?"

He said, "I went to sleep!"

I don't know a better place to sleep than around the altar. But we were all beating our brains out trying to get him filled, and he went to sleep on us. But that's the way we did things in those days. Sometimes I think it probably was more of a miracle that they got it at all. But they did. And, incidentally, I'm not finding fault with our old-timers in the faith, not at all. Bless their hearts; they at least did what they knew to do. That was more than anybody else knew. But we've learned some things since then. It doesn't make us any better. It just means we've learned more about the Scriptures. And it's right that we should.

Tarrying

The days of tarrying are over to receive the baptism of the Holy Spirit. Now the word "tarry" has no theological significance. It only means *wait*. And it is not a New Testament word. Anything before Acts 2 is not New Testament at all. So it only means to wait until the gift is given.

Some people have waited so long, and still have not received, that they've become discouraged in receiving the Holy Spirit. And you know what's happened? We haven't planned it this way. But unthinkingly, what has happened is that some of these people who have not received, who've been in the church so long, have begun to feel that there's something wrong with them. And some of the rest of the church think there's something wrong with them, too. Or else they'd get it. Finally, some of our good people begin to feel like second class citizens. Honey, I'm going to tell you something. There are no second class citizens with God. And the truth of the matter is, sometimes some of the worst people get it and don't live as good a life as the people who haven't got it. Don't say, "Amen," but you know it's right. But those who've got it wonder what's the matter with those who didn't. It doesn't mean they're second class citizens. It means they just haven't known how to yield. And that's what I'm here for—to tell you how.

Once, I was so pleased in a morning service when somebody came to me and said, "I'm one of the chronic seekers. I want to get it." I said, "You bet your life you're going to get it." Hallelujah! They will.

But that's what happened in our churches. I was in one place, one time. It was a good church. One Sunday night, 16 got the baptism in the Holy Spirit in one of our California cities. And one of the older men got it. And just in an encouraging way, I said, "Well thank God, brother, you've got it." This was in 1970. I said, "Thank God, you received it. How long have you been seeking?"

He said, "Since 1928."

I said, "Brother, that's 42 years."

He said, "I'm a charter member of the church."

Why do we let this happen? Well, we did.

In Juneau, a man who had been seeking for 40 years got the baptism in our meeting there. We showed him how to receive. This is the way it is. And so, everybody can get it.

My home is in the San Diego area of California, El Cajon to be exact, and we have a friend there. She is a Cherokee Indian lady, and comical and humorous. She just naturally is. One of those beady, black-eyed type, who looks you right in the eye and tells you what she thinks. And she ran a cleaning shop there. And I went in there once. She said, "You know what?"

I said, "No, what?"

She said, "When I was seeking for the Holy Ghost, I done everything they told me." She said, "I'd prayed so long and so hard one time, I began foaming at the mouth." Now, you know, that doesn't sound too bright! It doesn't sound too good, really. Then she said, "You know what?"

I said, "What?"

"I did that so long that I finally got fever blisters all over my mouth." She said, "so I told the Lord, 'If I gotta do this, I don't want it!'"

I said, "I don't blame you. I don't like fever blisters, myself."

Well, we've been through a lot of this kind of stuff, you know. And finally, someone showed them how to do it. There is no more Pentecost. I've heard people say, "Lord, give us another Pentecost." There's not going to be any more Pentecost. There was only one. That's a dispensational thing. And the Holy Spirit has been in the world since that time, and we can have it. Hallelujah!

Methods of Receiving

Now there are two ways God fills with the Holy Spirit. One is by **the laying on of hands**. Somebody like me or others comes along and preaches and prays and lays on hands, and people receive the Holy Spirit. That's one way. Then, another way is **the sovereign act of God**. Somebody might be praying and God just simply pours out the Holy Spirit, and they receive the Holy Spirit. That happens too.

Now when it comes to the laying on of hands, instruction is needed. I don't believe that the apostles went somewhere and just simply, all of a sudden, laid hands on people and people received the Holy Spirit. I don't think that at all. I think they took time to instruct the people on what would happen, what the phenomenon would be, and how to cooperate with God. And when they had prayer, they laid on hands; then the people received. I believe that.

Raymond T. Richey

Raymond T. Richey has gone to be with the Lord a long time ago. But I was with Richey many years ago in Florida. And he was one of the early men in divine healing. He was a man of great faith. I remember Richey telling people who would come to his meetings, "Before I will pray for you, you have to be in my meetings for three nights. It will take three nights to get out of your head what is wrong before I can get into your head what is right." And that's about where we are on the baptism in the Holy Spirit today. But, of course, I'm a little bolder. I'll try it the first night and find it works, too, as people believe. But it's no rush act, and there are no shortcuts to receiving. I think that Paul the Apostle must have had a little experience along this way, for he told Timothy "lay hands suddenly on no man" (I Tim. 5:22). It might not work.

Evangel College

I was at Evangel College in 1968. I was their speaker for spiritual emphasis week. And so I would speak every morning and every evening and sit in some of their classes during the day. Anybody who wanted to could attend the seminar and talk about this experience. And I was telling about all the things God did. Finally, one young student spoke up. I could tell she really had grit in her voice. She said to me, "Chaplain, you've told us all about your successes. Have you had any failures?"

I said, "Yes, I've had two or three failures, when people didn't do what I told them to do." So that stopped her. That bunch really froze up on me for a bit. But God finally got through to them, and 23 of them received the baptism in the Holy Spirit during our week we were with them. Hallelujah!

Matthew Henry

Matthew Henry had trouble in his days. He said that some were laying empty hands on empty heads and nobody was being benefited. So the problem is not new to us, really. It has come on down through the Church years.

False Expectations

You know, we Pentecostal people get funny ideas. If something unusual or out of this world would happen in Anchorage, they'd know it in Juneau before the night was over. And they'd know it on the East Coast by tomorrow. That's the way the word gets around among the Pentecostal people. I read somewhere one time where they were trying to get some little old lady filled with the Holy Spirit. And as they were praying, finally somebody thought she was about to get it. She said, "Hold on, sister, you're about to get it."

She opened her eyes big and wide and said, "No I ain't. I ain't blacked out yet."

Well, somewhere she got the idea you're supposed to black out. You're not supposed to black out.

I have blacked out in my life, and when I woke up, I was in the hospital or at home sick. And God doesn't do that to you to get you filled with the Holy Spirit. In Juneau one night, 11 got the baptism. To one man who got the baptism, I said, "Would you like to say a word to this bunch?"

He said, "Yes, the experience I had was, I didn't go unconscious."

Well, of course, not. But why do we think these kinds of things? We get a lot of funny ideas, don't we!

I was in another good church one time preaching on this, and I gave the altar call and I got ready to lay hands on one young man. But I heard him speaking in tongues. And I said, "Well, thank God, brother, you have it."

He stopped praying and he looked at me and said, "You know what?"

I said, "What?"

He said, "I've been doing this for two months and didn't know it."

I said, "Is that right?"

He said, "Yeah." After the meeting, he said, "Brother Linzey, let me tell you something. I don't know where I got this silly idea. But somewhere I got the idea that when I would receive the baptism of the Holy Spirit, the Holy Spirit would lift me off the floor 12 feet and I would go into orbit." Now the Bible doesn't say a thing about going into orbit. You don't go into orbit unless you are an astronaut and go with that bunch, you know! And that's not too religious of an experience, I don't think.

I talked to Al Warden, one of our astronauts, just a few days ago. And my wife asked Al Warden, "Did you think about God out there." He said, "No, we didn't get far enough out."

So I'm saying it wasn't too religious an experience. But here's what happens. And it hinders many people. Somehow, we get a preconceived notion or an idea of what God is going to do when we receive the Holy Spirit. Then we hold God accountable to do that. He is not accountable to do any dopey thing you have in your mind! Right? And if you haven't got the baptism in the Holy Spirit, how do you know what He's going to do? You can't hold Him accountable for some of your wild ideas. There's only one thing you're supposed to do. Anybody know what that is? Nobody knows? When you get the baptism what are you supposed to do? Nobody knows? Really? What's supposed to happen? My wife knows because she heard the lecture. You're supposed to speak in tongues. That's all you're supposed to do. And that's all the Bible says. Isn't that right? You thought I was going to trap you, didn't you? Nah, I'm not going to trap you. I'm just trying to get an answer to a question.

Falling Down

It's not necessary to have visions or fall down[4]. Some people think you have got to fall down all the time. Now I've got nothing against falling down. I've had people fall down in my meetings. But I don't expect this. And I don't stress this. I call it the domino theory. The first guy falls and about a million fall. And I'm not facetious. I mean, I just don't expect it. I think people do what they think they're supposed to do. And if the first guy falls, everybody thinks they have got to do it, too. But, you don't have to do that. No! Somebody once said, "Bless God, you will know when you get it!" Well, bless God, you might not! I just told you about the fellow who didn't know. How do you know you'll know when you get it? Another person said, "Well, because you'd really get great joy." Well, you might not! No joy is promised upon receiving the baptism with the Holy Spirit. The Bible doesn't talk about joy at all in that context.

Feelings

Do you know what happens? Do you know why we think you have to get great joy? Our people don't lie. But in testifying, they just don't tell the truth. A person will get the baptism on a Sunday night. They'll practice it every day. Then, maybe on Thursday, all of a sudden the joy will come. The joy will come sometime. It does. Then they'll come back to church on the next Sunday night and they'll say, "I received the Holy Spirit baptism and the joy flooded my soul." Well, that's true in a sense but not quite. They don't tell about the time lag or the time element involved. So the guy sitting next to him says, "Boy, it all happened at one time." And perhaps it did not. And so we need to understand that.

I was in one of the large churches down near where we live, and preaching on this subject. I was in the pastor's office before the meeting started. And one young married man was sitting there. He told me, "I hope tonight's the night. Every time we have a meeting, they tell me I'll get it this time. I haven't got it yet." Oh, and on and on and on, ad infinitum.

Finally, I said, "Well, if you do what I tell you to do, you'll get it."

So the meeting came, we laid on hands, and a number received the baptism. He did too, and he talked in tongues. But he wasn't happy with that. And like a big baby, he went out in the car and cried. I tell you the truth; I lie not. I didn't know this, but the pastor knew it. He went out and got a hold of him.

The young man said, "I thought I'd get it, and I didn't get it. I'm not happy."

And so the pastor said, "Why don't you go and talk to the Chaplain? He preached."

So he got him back in the office and he started crying and telling me, "Oh, but I thought it would be it." And he went on and on.

Finally, I said, "Shut up!" I said, "I'm more interested in you getting the baptism than you are, and Jesus is more interested than you." I said, "Even right now, if you would do it, I could lay hands on you again. If you'd open your mouth and talk, you'd have the baptism. Will you do it?"

He said, "Yes."

I said, "All right, receive the Holy Spirit." Boy, he opened his mouth and shouted out in tongues, and he jumped up out of his seat and ran around the pastor's desk about three times. Then he ran out into the sanctuary, up and down the aisles. Talk about getting it, he got it. Well, he finally did what the man of God said to do. And then he had to get on the telephone and call his people back in Indiana to tell them he had the baptism. Well he got the works that night. He got everything.

Well this is the way it is. Speaking in tongues, not feelings, not joy, is the evidence of receiving the Holy Spirit. And some of our critics will say, "But you people seek to speak in tongues." That's right. I make no apologies, of course. That's what we're talking about, isn't it! And so there we are.

Stammering Lips

Now when hands are laid on you, your lips will begin to tremble. We call this *stammering lips*, according to Isaiah 28:11. When hands are laid on you and your lips begin to tremble, if at that moment you would not hinder it, you would not stop it, you would not force yourself to speak English or any acquired language, you would exercise your faith, use your vocal cords and your mouth and your tongue and open your mouth and speak out by faith anything you did not know, you would be speaking in tongues in a matter of moments. This is the way it is. I've seen it happen over many thousands of times around the world in many, many nations. This is the way it is. Hallelujah! It is so simple, you will think you're doing it all by yourself. I've had people say to me afterwards, "I could have done this a long time ago." Of course, you could have. But you didn't know to do it, or for some reason you were afraid to do it.

You have the power to do it, or you have the power not to do it. First Corinthians 14:32 says, "the spirits of the prophets are subject to the prophets." This is a principle. Those of you who speak in tongues, you know you can talk in tongues any time you want to, don't you? Of course you do. And you can stop any time you want to, can't you? Of course you can. And so it is with receiving the initial evidence. You can do it if you will.

A Matter of the Will

It's a matter of the will. Now if you still want to tarry after hearing all of this, maybe somebody will tarry with you, but not I. However, I'll lay hands on you. If you'll follow me, you'll receive the Holy Spirit. One more example, then we'll close out this chapter.

I was preaching in Pasadena, California, some years ago, for the Full Gospel Businessmen's Fellowship banquet in the Pasadena Cafeteria, preaching on this subject. We had over a hundred people at the banquet. And after speaking, I gave the invitation for those who would like to receive the Holy Spirit to come forward. And a goodly number did. I did something that night I'd never done before. It showed that God was in it. The first party in line was a professional woman in business attire. I said, "When an infant is born into a family, he has no vocabulary. He cannot speak. But as he lives in the family, he knows mom and dad and the brothers and sisters. He picks up a word here and there—

"Daddy," "Mommy," and on and on. And as he lives in the family he keeps picking up words. And finally, he develops a vocabulary; it becomes meaningful to him, and he can speak. Tonight, when I lay hands on you, I will be speaking in tongues. Others will be speaking in tongues. If it will help you, there's no miracle in this, but if it will help you, take a word from me. It will be a word. It'll be my word. But take it, and don't be afraid to use it. Or if you have the faith, just open your mouth and say anything you want to. Do you understand this?"

Boy, she straightened herself up and looked at me and said, "Well, of course I understand you; I'm a language teacher." End of problem! I laid hands on her, and she received immediately, as everybody in line did that night.

Friends, here we are. This is the way it is. This is the door in, through which you enter.

Benediction

Heavenly Father, we give you thanks for your goodness to us, and your mercies that have been extended to us. Bless these people. Fill them with the Holy Spirit. Make this Church what you want it to be. In Jesus' name we pray. Amen.

3

CORNELIUS THE ROMAN CENTURION
ACTS 10

God is moving. It's wonderful what God is doing. And I'll tell you what—if we keep on like this, everybody will get filled, and everybody will begin to shout the glory a little bit and praise God. We'll have a revival. This is revival when things like this begin to happen.

Some people just don't learn to pray out loud. It's always kind of turned in, and they whisper. Why do that? God gave you vocal cords. Most of you can't talk in church, but when you get home, people can hear you three blocks away yelling at the kids. So don't be afraid to talk out in church, you know? Talk it out. It'll do something for your personality. You need to express yourself. It will make you an outgoing personality. That's the way it is.

Review

Now in chapters one and two, we dealt with Joel 2:28 and Acts 1 and Acts 2, both of which talk about the outpouring of the Holy Spirit. Really, that's the only outpouring of the Holy Spirit. I've heard people say, "Lord, give us another Pentecost." He's not going to do it. There's only one Pentecost, and that took place nearly 2,000 years ago when the Holy Spirit was given. And since that time, the Holy Spirit has always been in the world. And now every time men and women, boys or girls, get saved, they receive the Holy Spirit. And then if they knew to do so, and had not been trained against it, they could immediately receive the infilling of the Holy Spirit and speak in tongues. It would be that simple. And that's the way the Lord meant for it to be. We discuss these things in Acts 1 and Acts 2.

Regeneration or the Baptism with the Holy Spirit

Now before we go on to Acts 10, there are a couple of statements I want to make here. R.A. Torrey, the noted Baptist scholar, made these statements. The baptism of the Holy Spirit is an operation of the Holy Spirit distinct from and subsequent to and additional to his regenerating work. A man may be regenerated by the Holy Spirit and still not be baptized with the Holy Spirit. In regeneration there's an importation of life, and the one who receives it is saved. In the baptism of the Holy Spirit there's an importation of power and the one who receives it is fitted for service. Every true believer has the Holy Spirit. Now that's according to Romans 8:9. You ought to memorize Romans 8:9, which says, "But ye are not in the flesh, but in the Spirit, if so be that the Spirit of God dwells in you. Now if any man have not the Spirit of Christ, he is none of His." So every believer has the Holy Spirit. But not every believer has the baptism of the Holy Spirit, though he could have. The baptism of the Holy Spirit may be received immediately after the new birth. An example is the household of Cornelius. And that's what we're going to discuss here.

In the normal state of the Church, every believer would have the baptism of the Holy Spirit as in the church at Corinth. In such a normal state of the Church, the baptism of the Holy Spirit would be received immediately upon repentance and baptism into the name of Jesus Christ for the remission of sins. But the doctrine of the baptism of the Holy Spirit has been sold out to drop out of sight, and the Church has had so little expectancy along this line for its young children, that a large portion of the Church is in the position of the churches in Samaria and Ephesus, where someone has to come and call the attention of the mass of believers to their privilege in the risen Christ and claim it for them. And that's what I'm doing in these kinds of meetings—claiming it for you.

Now, as R.A. Torrey said, in a normal state of the Church, believers would receive the Holy Spirit baptism just like they did in the household of Cornelius or like they did throughout the book of Acts. It's amazing. We Pentecostal people are very quick in talking to denominational people and will very quickly tell them what Acts 2:39 says, "For the promise is unto you, and to your children, and to all that are afar off, even as many as the Lord our God shall call." Now that's Scripture and that's correct. The promise is to everybody. That's true. But while we go to all lengths and all extremes to point that out to everybody else, why do we overlook Acts 2:38, the verse just ahead of it? It reads like this, "Peter said unto them, 'Repent, and be baptized every one of you in the name of Jesus Christ for the remission of sins, and ye shall receive the gift of the Holy Ghost.'" Why don't we make something out of that one? That one is just as important as the other one is.

The Sailor from Long Beach Naval Shipyards

Now I was in a small church in Southern California some time ago preaching on the baptism of the Holy Spirit. It was a very small church. Maybe it would have seated 50. I preached in the morning; then I preached that evening. And so that evening, when I gave the call for those who wanted to come forward to receive the baptism, a sailor and an elderly man came forward. We were near the Long Beach Naval Shipyards. And so the sailor could get to the church. But his noble idea for being in church that night was that he was going with one of the girls in the assembly. That's why he was in church. But he heard me preach that morning and heard me preach that night.

So when I gave the call to come forward, the sailor and the elderly man got up and came right down the middle aisle, wanting to receive the Holy Spirit. Now since someone in the church knew that I, the evangelist, did not know the situation with the sailor, and wanting to be sure that the evangelist got the word, somebody in the back of the church cupped her hands and, in a hoarse whisper that you could hear all over the little old church, she said, "He's not even saved." Everybody got the word that the sailor wasn't saved. I got it and everybody else, except the sailor. He must not have got it, or he didn't know what she was talking about. He was a Catholic lad and had never received Jesus Christ. But all he knew was he wanted the Holy Spirit. And so here he is now standing in front of me. I was in uniform that night and so was he. So he was standing at attention. I now knew he's not saved because I got the word. But what am I going to do? I had promised the sailor and anybody who came forward that they would receive the Holy Spirit. So I'm going to keep my word. I looked that sailor straight in the eyes. I said, "Son, would you receive the Holy Spirit if I laid hands on you?"

He said, "Yes sir!"

I reached over and put my hands on that Catholic sailor's head and I said, "Receive the Holy Spirit."

He had his hands down to his side. And when I said, "Receive the Holy Spirit," he bowed his head, and he squinted his face like he was in excruciating pain.

All of a sudden, he threw both hands to heaven and he cried out to God, "Save me, save me!" And he began talking in tongues.

He got saved and got the whole works like he was supposed to. He didn't know any differently. He got what he was supposed to get. There was only one thing about that. We didn't put him through the old "one, two, three" routine like we do in our Pentecostal and Charismatic churches. You know, "Everybody bow your heads, don't anybody look now, just raise your hands." Well, I don't do that any more. You can watch everything I do. I have nothing to hide. You can look me right in the eye as I talk right to you.

The point is, the sailor came forward. All he knew was that he wanted God. That's all he knew. And God dealt with him. And in just a few seconds he got the whole thing right there. Undoubtedly, a conversion took place because God doesn't fill people that are not saved! Isn't that right? Sure it's right.

The Baptism and Salvation

Somebody said to me one time, "But you've got to be careful. Suppose they get the baptism and aren't saved." Oh come on! Get off of it! We got better sense than that, haven't we? Somebody said one time, "You've got to be careful the way you do it. They might speak in tongues and not have the Holy Ghost." Come on! That's just not too bright to talk like that. But some people talk like that, you know. But here's the sailor that got the whole works at one time.

That's the way it ought to be. And if we could teach that to people, they would understand that. They could receive the Holy Spirit just like when they get saved, and that would be God's plan for them to do so. It's not His plan that we spend time and time and time tarrying to receive the Holy Spirit, not since the Holy Spirit has been given. Say me a good "Amen" to that.

Cornelius the Roman Centurion

Now we're going over to Acts 10 to take a look at Cornelius. I like the story of Cornelius because it's the story of a military man. I really love that. I'll tell you for sure. Somebody said to me one time, "You know, if you're a Christian, how can you be a chaplain in the Navy?" Somebody had a gripe about the military. I said, "Really, that's your problem and not mine." I've never had any problem with it.

But here's the story of a military man. God loved him and God saved him and God filled him. We have no record that he ever got out of the military. He belonged to the Roman army. Now I realize here that you're not supposed to give any private interpretation to Scriptures. But I do have a private one on that one, which I'm going to pass on to you, about why he stayed in the military. Probably he didn't have his 20 years in yet. But then, I won't push the point on that one.

Now I'm not going to read you the whole story. You can read that yourself this evening. But the story is this. Here is Cornelius, a man who loved God, and a convert to Judaism. In those days, to be saved, you had to be converted to Judaism. And he was a proselyte. He did all he knew to do until, finally, one day he fasted and prayed, gave alms to the people, and the angel of the Lord met with him and really shook him up. And the angel told Cornelius to send down to Joppa and get Simon Peter who was dwell with Simon the Tanner. He'll come up and tell you what you and your household should do that they might be saved. And so Cornelius sent two servants and a soldier down there to get Peter to come up and talk to him. Now about the time the servants got down to where Peter was, Peter had gone on the housetop to pray. That would be like going on the back porch down in our country. And he's waiting for a meal, and the Scripture says he was very hungry. Somebody was still getting the meal ready.

And so while he was up there he fell into a trance. Now what is more normal and natural than being hungry and falling into a trance and thinking of something to eat? And so he saw a vision of a sheet let down from Heaven. And all manner of beasts were in it—unclean, of course. And then he heard a voice say, "Rise, Peter; kill and eat."

And the bigoted Jew says, "Not so, Lord; for I have never eaten any thing that is common or unclean."

And the voice says, "What God hath cleansed, that call not thou common" (Acts 10:13-15).

This happened three times, and then the sheet was drawn up into Heaven again. And about that time, the men approached the house, there's a rap on the door, and the Spirit told Peter that three men were seeking him, and that he should go down there and go with them and don't doubt anything. And so Peter went down and greeted them and brought them into the house. And they told him what the situation was. And the Scripture says the next day they went up to Caesarea, and they met at Cornelius's house.

Now, in anticipation of what God was going to do, Cornelius invited all of his family and friends together. They had a house full of people up there. That's New Testament Christianity. You invite everybody and get to see that they get the Word. And when Peter arrived, Cornelius fell on his face before Peter, and Peter raised him up and said, "Stand up. I'm a man just as you are." What is it that you want? And Cornelius told Peter the story again. Remember I had said previously that in the Old Testament dispensation it appears that God was a respecter of people. And then Peter says in Acts 10:34-35, "...of a truth I perceive that God is no respecter of persons: but in every nation he that feareth Him, and worketh righteousness, is accepted with Him."

Now God has revealed to Peter that there is no difference between the Jew and the Gentile, that God loves everybody and wants to save everybody, and anybody who has a mind to do right—God is with him. That's the gist of this text, if you please.

And then you notice another thing. When Cornelius tells his story, this also has given a reason for Peter to preach the gospel. I brought to your attention in the last chapter that if you read the Bible through, something always has to happen to give a preacher a reason to preach. And so, when this took place here, this gave Peter a reason to preach. And so he begins then. And after these verses, he begins to preach Jesus Christ to the Gentiles. And he really lays it on them, including how and why Christ came and died and rose again.

Receiving through the Direct Sovereign Will of God

Now, after having said all this and having preached the sermon, no altar call was given. No conclusion was drawn. In verses 44 to 48 the Scripture reads,

While Peter yet spake these words, the Holy Spirit fell on all them which heard the Word. And they of the circumcision which believed were astonished, as many as came with Peter, because that on the Gentiles also was poured out the gift of the Holy Spirit. For they heard them speak with tongues, and magnify God. Then answered Peter, 'Can any man forbid water, that these should not be baptized, which have received the Holy Spirit as well as we?' And he commanded them to be baptized in the name of the Lord.

Now Peter is preaching Jesus Christ to these people, and while he is still preaching, God sends out the Holy Spirit upon them, and here they're speaking in tongues. Everybody has received the infilling of the Holy Spirit. Now, here, they were concurrently converted and filled with the Spirit. I frankly believe this is the New Testament pattern. And why we in Pentecostal circles have digressed from this pattern, I don't understand. It happened this way at Pentecost. It happened this way in Acts 10. It happened this way in Acts 19. It happened this way in Acts 8. How did we ever separate the experience? It beats anything I ever heard. But we managed to do it.

Well I shouldn't be so unkind. We really didn't manage to do it. God was good enough to us in the turn of the century to come down and give us an outpouring of the Holy Spirit, if you please, and bring to our attention that this is part and parcel of the total, genuine conversion experience. And it is. Hallelujah! You see, I've come to the place now that I believe all Christians can talk in tongues. I believe that. I have no trouble with that at all. Based on Acts 2:38, I believe they can do it. Some people don't like that kind of thinking. But that's the way it is. And if you find out differently, you let me know. But, otherwise, I'll stay with what I found out, okay? Fine! Thank you!

Now here he's still preaching, and the Holy Spirit is given. We've made it so difficult. Oh, have we made it difficult! "Brother, you've got to be so holy." The way that we get so holy! Honey, if you've got to get as holy as we want you to get, you won't need it anyway. Right? Sure! But I'll save that for the next chapter.

But here he's still preaching on the Holy Spirit, and they ended up speaking in tongues. Now you know, Peter was pretty bright. But I've never seen a dumb Jew, yet. Really! Have you? No, they're all pretty bright. Peter had an idea that when he went down to Caesarea, or up to Caesarea, that something was going to go wrong. He could tell it. So he grabbed about six Christian Jews and took them with him. He didn't want to be caught over there by himself, with the Gentiles. That's bad business. And so when the Holy Spirit was given, here he was with six Christian Jews who heard and saw the evidence of what took place. You know, that's what I do in the meetings I have here. If someone speaks in tongues, I'll call somebody else around to hear, so there are witnesses that someone received it. In case that person gets discouraged and says, "No I didn't," the witness can say, "Yes you did. We heard you." That's the reason for it, of course. Because, sometimes, people who have the Holy Spirit don't really know they have it, it takes somebody to tell them they have got it. You didn't know that, did you! But that's right. And so we tell you that you have it, and we try to get someone to be a witness. Peter had six Christian Jews up there with him, and they heard and saw this whole thing. It says, "And they of the circumcision which believed were astonished, as many as came with Peter, because that on the Gentiles also was poured out the gift of the Holy Spirit" (Acts 10:45). These believing Jews, the Christian Jews, were with him, and they heard them speak in tongues.

Trouble with the Church Leaders in Jerusalem

Now Peter was right. Trouble was brewing, because, just as soon as the church in Jerusalem heard that Peter had been up to see the Gentiles, this caused no little stir. They convened a general council immediately to talk to Peter. Now I want to tell you when you're big enough to have a special general council called for you, you're a pretty big man. But Peter was a big man. So a special general council was convened. No matter what they did, Jerusalem always got the word. Jerusalem got the word of what Peter did and they called him on the carpet. And, oh, the charge they had on

Peter. Do you know what the charge was? Eating with the Gentiles! Terrible, huh? They called him on the carpet!

Witnesses

Well Peter was ready for them. He got the six Christian Jews. I would imagine he said to them, "Fellows, there's trouble in Jerusalem. Come on down with me. We gotta talk to them there." So they went up to Jerusalem and he told the whole story of the vision and meeting with Cornelius. Then he said, in Acts 11:15-18, "As I began to speak, the Holy Spirit fell on them, as on us at the beginning. Then remembered I the word of the Lord, how that He said, 'John indeed baptized with water; but ye shall be baptized with the Holy Spirit.' Forasmuch then as God gave them the like gift as He did unto us, who believed on the Lord Jesus Christ, what was I, that I could withstand God?' When they heard these things, they held their peace, and glorified God, saying, 'then hath God also to the Gentiles granted repentance unto life.'"

Now this is the crux of the whole thing. "As I began to speak, the Holy Spirit fell on them, as on us at the beginning." And the beginning is Pentecost in Acts 2. That's where the Holy Spirit was given. They realized what took place because they had the same phenomenon, the speaking in tongues, as the Holy Spirit prompted them. In verse 16, "Then remembered I the word of the Lord." Jesus said the Holy Spirit, the Comforter, shall bring all things to your remembrance whatsoever I have said unto you (John 14:26). And here Peter says, "Then remembered I the word of the Lord, how that He said, 'John indeed baptized with water; but ye shall be baptized with the Holy Spirit.'" He called this thing at Cornelius's house the baptism with the Holy Spirit. Is this clear? It's what He said.

Consistency

Now this lines up with Matthew 3:11. John said, "I indeed baptize you with water unto repentance; but . . . He shall baptize you with the Holy Spirit, and with fire." The next verse is Acts 1:5, where Jesus said, "Ye shall be baptized with the Holy Spirit not many days hence." Then Acts 2 came, where it says they were baptized with the Holy Spirit. Then Peter went down to Cornelius's house, and he said, "Then remembered I the word of the Lord, how that He said, 'John indeed baptized with water; but ye shall be baptized with the Holy Spirit.'" Peter calls this occasion the baptism with the Holy Spirit.

Terminology

Now my question to the Baptists always is, "If He called this the baptism with the Holy Spirit, and this is the third time that term is used, why would the baptism with the Holy Spirit not be the same today as it was in the early Church? We say it is the same. We say we're part and parcel of the Early Church. We say we're part of the New Testament Church. We say we're in the Church Age or the Holy Spirit dispensation. If that be true, then whatever took place in the beginning of a dispensation has to hold throughout the dispensation, until God makes a change. And so again, this is called the baptism with the Holy Spirit. This is AD 41, probably some eight years after the Day of Pentecost.

Well Peter certainly defended himself very well there. And, again, we see that the same phenomenon took place in Caesarea that took place at Pentecost—they spoke with tongues. Now this is the second Scripture we have which says they spoke with tongues.

I was speaking with a friend one time. And he didn't believe in any of these phenomena. But when I mentioned Acts 2, he said, "Well, sure, but don't you realize that the Holy Spirit was just given to the Jews there?"

I said, "Well, that's right." Then I thought that if you're going to win an argument, you've got to act a little dumb. If you're too bright he won't argue with you. So I asked, "But what about Acts 10?"

He said, "Let's read it."

I said, "Yeah, let's."

And we examined Acts 10 where God took the Gentiles in, too. Now if that were all the Scripture we had, that would be sufficient. But then we also have the baptism with the Holy Spirit in Acts 19, which we'll examine in the next chapter. But the Jews have been taken in, and the Gentiles have been received. And according to the third chapter of Ephesians, we find out that the Jew and Gentile, both, make up God's Church. Now we've got them all in the fold, saved and filled with the Holy Spirit. So it's not just for the Jews.

Practical Factors: Cooperating with God in Speaking

Now, let us go for a little bit to discuss some practical factors here. I remember when I was in one church in Juneau. One lady came to an altar and received the Holy Spirit. She came down very primly with her little Testament in her hand. I said, "Would you lay your Bible on the table?" And she did. And so I said, "All right, now you love the Lord, and you already have the Holy Spirit. Raise your hands, begin speaking in tongues." Well, she looked like she was going to cry.

She said, "I don't want to do it, I want Him to do it."

I said, "Honey, he ain't gonna do it. You gotta do it." And she began speaking in tongues, just like that.

It's funny how we do things. We just want to come and stand like automatons or icons or statues or something, and make God come down and get us going. He doesn't do that. He does not violate your will. He does not violate your mind—not at all. He invites your cooperation. If you do what He suggests you do, you move right on in. This is putting faith in the operation! This is how you receive! We hear so much on yielding to God and none of us know what *yield* means. I don't know what it means. How do you yield? I don't know. Have faith! How do you do it? I don't know.

All I know to do is open your mouth and do it. That's having faith. Hallelujah! I wish they'd quit writing books once in a while. They muddy the water. Just do it!

Quit talking so much about faith and just do it! Put faith into practice. Put faith into action. "But I don't want to. I want it to be God." That's sounds noble, doesn't it? Honey, if you talk in tongues, it'll be God. Don't you worry about it!

Can You Make a Mistake?

The question sometimes arises, when you are speaking in tongues, can you make a mistake? My reply is, "Who do you think you are?" Somebody said to me one time, "I'm afraid I might make a mistake!" I said, "How would you know?" Well we think we know a lot, don't we? We really don't know anything. But be that as it may. When hands are laid on you, your lips will being to stammer or tremble. We call that in Isaiah 28, stammering lips. I've seen it time and time again. You've seen people in the prayer room whose lips begin to tremble. If they would, they could just go ahead and talk in tongues. But they don't know what's going on. So they say, "dadadada," and on and on and on, ad infinitum, ad nauseum. Right?

My wife, Verna Linzey, brought that up the other day. I thought it was pretty good. When a man can realize his wife says something good once in a while, it's pretty good. But we know a party down in a small church where we go once in a while where we live. There's a lady in the church. And she'll get stirred up once in a while. In the middle of a service she'll stand and say, "dadadadada." That's all she ever does.

If it's not my church, I don't have a right to go in and set it straight. That's not my prerogative. The pastor ought to do it, but he doesn't know to do it. One of these days I'm going to just tell him, "Why don't you do something about it?" But Verna suggested that when a kid learns to talk, he learns to say "Dada" or "Mommy," or something like that. Some never get past the stage of "dadadadadada." Why don't you begin with "Dadada," and grow up and go on and talk in tongues? You could if you would.

But we in Pentecost have been a beat down bunch of people. We've been hammered down so badly. It's a wonder that we all don't have twisted, crooked personalities that are bent out of shape, or something. We're afraid to exert ourselves. We're afraid to say anything, for it might be wrong. We don't know what "rightness" is. We're afraid anything we do might be wrong. Why don't we break out of the shell and do anything? Be a live personality, an outgoing personality, a whole personality, and have an integrated mind, if you please. That's what this is all about. Hallelujah! Okay, I don't want to get over your head. But that's the way it is.

English or Other Tongues?

Don't make yourself speak English if you want to receive the Holy Spirit and speak in tongues. You know, it's a psychological fact and a physiological fact that you can only speak one language at a time. Try speaking two of them and see what happens. Impossible! So, if you're going to make yourself speak English or any other acquired language, that's all you should try to speak. But if, by faith, you refuse to speak a language that you know and just open your mouth and blurt out anything else, you'll be speaking in tongues. This is a faith message from beginning to end. Why don't you try it and find out and see how it works. You'd be surprised. Really, it's so simple, you'll think you're doing it all by yourself. Somebody told me after one meeting, "Well, I'm just imitating you." I said, "Fine! Keep it up. It sounds good."

We've been so afraid to imitate. Somebody once said, "Don't you imitate!" But Paul said, "Imitate me as I imitate Christ" (I Cor. 11:1 NASB). It's a good way to get started. We need to be readers of the Bible. And many of us are. But most of us don't read too much, and, instead, we hear what everybody else says. Go ahead. You have the power to do it.

Is It Me or Is It God?

Somebody once said, "I'm afraid it might be me."

I said, "Well it won't be your twin brother."

Of course it'll be you if you talk in tongues. What do you think? And if it's not you, I'm getting out of here, fast!

The Power to Speak in Tongues

Now you have the power to speak in tongues or you have the power to resist speaking in tongues. You are the one who operates your spirit! "And the spirits of the prophets are subject to the prophets" (I Cor. 14:32). Somebody said one time, "Well, when the power comes down, I can't control it!" You're mistaken! If you can't control it, you got something else. For we all control our own spirit. It's scriptural. If you can't control your spirit, they lock you up. That's what they have those people down there for. Someone told me today about somebody who thought he was the king of England. They got him in an asylum down there, just 'cause he thinks he's the king. Well that's the way it is. Sure, you have the power to control your own spirit. You have the power! You control you! I control me! I can speak in tongues any time I want. I can stop any time I want.

Coast Guardsman

Do you know what I did one time? I was attending the senior chaplain school in Newport, Rhode Island, in 1970 to 1971. We were meeting and working with people on the streets as part of a ministry assignment. I went into a Christian Men's Service Center. A young man there was troubled. So he was trying to find an Assembly of God chaplain. He belonged to an Assembly of God church in New York. So someone said, "There's an Assembly of God chaplain." And just as soon as I got there he came over and asked, "Are you an Assembly of God chaplain?"

I said, "Yes, I am."

"Are you, really?"

I said, "Yes, I really am."

He said, "Can I talk to you?"

I said, "Sure, you can."

And he had a real story to tell. Well it was so long I could see that he needed more than just ten minutes. And he needed fellowship worse than anything. He was a Coast Guard sailor. He had come up on the Cutter from New York to Newport for the yacht races. The Coast Guard Cutter always comes up, and he was a cook on the Cutter. And so I took him with me all down through Newport. Then I invited him home that evening for dinner with my wife and children. And he said, "Now can I talk to you?"

I said, "Yes."

Well he was heavily burdened and distressed. He said, "If I can just talk in tongues, it would do me so much good."

I said, "Oh, but you can."

He said, "Oh, no I can't!"

I said, "Well, of course, you can."

He said, "The only time I can do it is when the power comes on."

I said, "Well, how do you get the power on?" Well, he didn't know. I said, "I'm going to show you something." I said, "Now, here's what I'm going to do. When I count to three, you raise your hands immediately and start talking in tongues."

He said, "I can't do it."

I said, "Will you try?"

"Yes."

I said, "Okay, get ready! One, two, three, go!" And we both started talking in tongues. And he looked around. I said, "Stop, stop!"

And he stopped and put his hands down. He said, "I didn't know I could do this!"

I said, "Sure, you can do it. And just to show you can, we're going to do it again. Okay, get ready. One, two, three, go!" We both started talking in tongues, again. I said, "Okay, stop!" And he stopped.

He said, "I didn't know it worked like this."

I said, "Okay, you found out something, didn't you?"

"Yeah!"

I said, "Now, you practice this in your private daily prayer life, no matter where you are." And he said he would.

Well, that must have been in September or October of 1970. And so then the races were over, and the Coast Guard Cutter went back to New York. At Christmas time, I got a card from him. "Dear Chaplain, Merry Christmas! Since I met with you and found out I could speak with tongues, I have practiced it every day. And now the Lord has given me several languages, and I speak in tongues." Now, this is the way it was. He didn't know he could do this. He was waiting for somebody to turn the power on. Nobody's going to do it. Honey, you have to turn your own power on. That's why the Lord gave it to you. "But ye shall receive power, after that the Holy Spirit is come upon you" (Acts 1:8). You've got the power!

Our problem is we don't want the responsibility for the power. Honey, you've got the responsibility whether you want it or not! And you don't blame God for anything that goes wrong! And you don't blame God for not getting the job done! You have the responsibility! That's the way God will have it. Glory to God! So this responsibility has been delegated to us.

Step Out by Faith

A step of faith is necessary. We Pentecostal people talk more about faith and have less of it than anybody I know. We don't have much faith. We're always waiting for God to do something. Ours is a "gimme" religion. "Gimme, gimme, gimme!" That's the kind of religion we've got. Instead of acting on faith and acting like real men and women with maturity, we act like kids—always crying for something. Don't we? Yeah, we do.

All I'm trying to do is give you a little faith, show you how to operate, tell you to use and show you how to use what you've got. "If ye then, being evil, know how to give good gifts unto your children, how much more shall your heavenly Father give the Holy Spirit to them that ask him?" (Luke 11:13). Many have been asking and keep asking and still haven't had it because they don't receive it. Don't blame God. He's ready. And he expects us to cooperate.

Does the Holy Spirit Speak Through You?

I have heard people say that when a person speaks in tongues, the Holy Spirit speaks through him. Now that sounds holy, doesn't it? It just isn't true! That's the only trouble with that statement. What do you think we are? Zombies? Automatons or robots? No, He doesn't do that. The Holy Spirit does not take over anybody and make them do anything. Not at all! The Roman Catholic version provides the best reading of Acts 2:4. It states, "They began to speak with other tongues as the Holy Spirit prompted them." They did the speaking. The Holy Spirit prompted them.

Let's look at this a little further. Somebody once said, "But when you talk in tongues, that's God talking." No it isn't! And just to bring this to your attention, what about in I Corinthians 14 where Paul sets the church in order for the misuse of tongues? Brother, if it was God, you can't set anything in order, because God wouldn't make any mistakes. Paul the Apostle said, "If any man speak in an unknown tongue, let it be by two, or at the most three" (I Cor. 14:27). And that's all! Now, if this is God, nobody can tell

God how much He's going to talk! But he tells us no more than two or three. And then let there be an interpreter. And if there's no interpreter, let him keep silence in the church. You can't tell God to keep silence in the church, if this is God. I'm just telling you it's for sure that it's not God. It's our own spirit that's operating in this kind of a vein. And we have a responsibility to see that we know what we're doing. Hallelujah!

So we must begin to speak in tongues. We have the power to do it, for remember that "The spirits of the prophets are subject to the prophets" (I Cor. 14:32). We can control our own spirits. Therefore, we know we have to keep order in the church. We control ourselves. By faith one must open his mouth. And you know it's a physiological fact that you can't talk with your mouth closed. But I've seen people come and try to speak in tongues with their mouths closed. I guess they think God's going to pry it open, maybe, and do it for them. But He's not. He's not going to do it. You have to want the Holy Spirit baptism. You have to want what God has for you. You have to want to come down and cooperate with the Lord that you might receive the baptism. Hallelujah! And then the manifestation is what you speak.

He gives the ability for utterance, but you do the speaking. Keep your mouth and your lips in action and your voice loud. We've got a lot of whisperers today. They come down to the altar and hardly make a sound. Why don't you put your voice to it? You don't have to whisper to God. Put your voice to it. I've got a mother and dad. They're Baptist. And they know how the Pentecostals yell and shout a little bit. And my mother said one time about the shouting, "God's not deaf, you know." I said, "No, and He's not nervous either." Open your mouth and talk to Him. The point is that it does something for your spirit to speak out. And that's the thing we're concerned with.

Now with some people, once they hear themselves say a couple of words, then they go quiet; they stop, and then they forget to talk. No, keep on. Somebody said to me one time, "You mean we're not supposed to concentrate?" How can you concentrate when you don't know what you're going to say? How can you? This is a non-intellectual exercise, if you please. It bypasses the intellect.

The Lady Who Couldn't Speak in Tongues—but Did Anyway

I was in one church one time and they gave the call to the people who wanted to receive the baptism. One lady came down. So I told the lady, "When I lay hands on your head, open your mouth and begin to speak in tongues." And so I laid hands on her head.

Then she got into this routine thing of saying, "I love you Jesus, I love you Jesus, I love you Jesus," and on and on and on, and wouldn't stop. But, what was worse, I couldn't get her to pay attention any more.

Finally, I said, "Stop!" And boy she stopped. I said, "He knows you love Him. You're not telling Him anything new. Why don't you talk in tongues?"

She said, "But I can't."

I said, "You can."

"I can't." We had a little argument down there.

I said, "Sure, you can. Now, I'll lay hands on you again."

And I did. Finally, she got her courage up; she opened her mouth and began to speak in tongues. That's the way it is, and that's how easy it is. Hallelujah!

How Much Speaking Is Required to Receive the Baptism?

The question has been asked, "How much speaking is required to receive the baptism?" There's no criterion on how much speaking one must do. I've been in places where somebody talked in tongues and somebody said, "Well, what if we let him talk a long time to be sure he really got it?" Well how much talking are you supposed to do? The Bible doesn't say, "Talk two hours to prove it." Willard Cantelon was one of the finest evangelists in the Assemblies of God, and one of the finest preachers on the baptism in the Holy Spirit. But Cantelon made this statement one time. He was preaching in Quebec, French Canada. And an English Canadian came down to get the baptism. He laid hands on her. And she said one word, the French word for God which is 'Dieu.' Cantelon said she received the Holy Spirit. I believe that. Now, of course, she'll go ahead and put it into practice. She'll speak more and that'll develop. But there's no certain amount one has to speak in tongues. Hallelujah!

Forgetting Your Words

In Juneau, in a question and answer period, someone asked the question, "When you receive the Holy Spirit, what if you forget the words you had?" I said, "Don't worry about it. Get some new ones."

The little Cherokee lady down home where we live had a husband named Gano. She was sewing at their house one night about midnight. These are the kind of people who believe that if you say, "God told me," brother, that's everything. That's it. You don't question it. If you say, "God said," that's right! No question! And she said to us, "The Lord talked to me and told me that if I would get my husband out of bed and lay hands on him, he would receive the Holy Ghost."

I said, "Is that right?"

She said, "Yes." So she said, "Gano!" He was in bed asleep.

He said, "What?"

She said, "The Lord told me, if you'll get up, you'll get the baptism."

"He did?"

"Yeah."

"Okay."

Boy, he come climbing out of bed. And she laid hands on him, and he got two words and went around the house shouting those two words out. That's a baptism. Then he went back to bed. Then the next morning they got up. He couldn't remember his two words! He lost them. Oh, he couldn't remember them for nothing. It was just terrible. And he was so dejected. I think she laid hands on him again and got them back. Well we people do funny things, don't we? But that's the way it worked with those people, you see.

I was in one of our fine churches in Southern California. And a young Mexican man, fine young fellow, a very intelligent young man, came running down to the altar. I laid hands on him so he could speak in tongues. I thought I did something wrong when a deacon said, "You have to watch that fellow. He speaks three languages, fluently." I could see that the deacon was afraid the young man was pulling one on us. So I grabbed the young man by the lapels and said, "Hey, stop! Do you understand what you're saying?" He smiled and said, "No, I don't know this one." God had filled him with the Holy Spirit.

Spiritual Hang Ups

I'll have to tell you this one. I think this is the cutest thing that ever happened. I was in one church, and my we had a good meeting. We had a houseful of people. Quite a number had received the Holy Spirit, and we were about to close the meeting out. And two elderly little ladies came down the middle aisle. And the pulpit was not too high. The first little elderly lady said, "Chaplain?"

I said, "Yes?

She said, "I received the Holy Ghost Sunday night, but I can't talk in tongues any more."

"Yes, you can."

"No, I can't."

"Yes, you can."

"No, I can't."

The little lady with her was the one who helped. She said, "Chaplain, what she would like to tell you is, all she can say is, 'Glub, glub.'"

Well, that doesn't sound too bright does it? If my Harvard colleagues could hear me talking this kind of language, they'd say, "Well, Linzey, he really went out, didn't he?"

I said, "All right. When I lay hands on you, you say, 'Glub, glub.'"

She said, "All right." So I laid hands on her and she said, "Glub, glub."

And after about the second "Glub," she was off talking in tongues and having the time of her life. Now, that's comical. We get hung up on some of the most little, inconsequential things. You know, really, if all I could say was "Glub, glub," that would sound stupid, wouldn't it? I could hardly face myself in the mirror and say, "Glub, glub." It doesn't sound bright. And this little lady felt like that—kind of stupid, you know? And she was so embarrassed that she couldn't even tell me. The little friend had to tell me. When she could see that I accepted her saying, "Glub, glub," she could accept herself, and not feel ashamed or stupid. And then when she could do that, she forgot all about saying, "Glub, glub," and went ahead and talked in tongues.

But there are a lot of people at our churches who are hung up just on stupid little things like that. I've heard people say a couple of words in tongues, and then say, "Oh, that's nothing. I made that up." And they treat it that way. And because they treat it that way, they think it's stupid, and they don't go on with it. The point is, if you don't know anything, then learn something! This is the thing I'm trying to pass on. This is not particularly brilliant. These are just things I found out by experience. And I found that it has helped people around the world. People get hung up on things. When they realize what little things hang them up, then they're free to go ahead and express themselves.

All Utterances Have Meaning

First Corinthians 14:10 states, "There are, it may be, so many kinds of voices in the world, and none of them is without signification." That means any thing you would utter would have a meaning to it as far as God is concerned. Anything you would have to utter would have significance to it. This has been there all the time. We fail to see these things, and we need to understand them.

All believers have the Holy Spirit. You have the power and you have the ability to speak in tongues. And you know how children learn to speak. They listen to parents and others. I always say in my meetings, "If you want to, take a word from me or take a word from anybody speaking in tongues just to get started. There's no magic in it. Not at all. If you take a word from me, it won't be your word; it'll be my word. But just take it so you can learn how to get free and use your mouth and use your tongue. After all, this is an exercise in faith, isn't it? The church isn't going to bust open, the clouds aren't going to send a shower with lightning from heaven and an earthquake. But we think everything's going to happen. All of a sudden the power's going to drop when we talk in tongues. It just doesn't work that way, that's all. The next thing is to learn how to cooperate and work with God, so God can move in and through you and with you. Hallelujah!

This is the way it is, and we need to understand it. There's no reason for tarrying to receive the Holy Spirit. The Holy Spirit has already been given. The thing we do now is cooperate in the reception. And what little you speak, accept it as of God, and move on from that point. Despise not the day of small beginnings. And once you speak in tongues, practice it in your daily private prayer life 'til it becomes just a part of your own very nature. I drive down the streets speaking in tongues and having a big time because it does not take the mental processes to do so. It's not a mental exercise at all. It's a spiritual exercise, and that's all you can say for it. Hallelujah! And so this is the way it is.

Benediction

Father, we thank you for your goodness to us, and your kindness, for your word which teaches us how to be filled. Give us faith to believe you. Give us faith to accept your word, and to act upon that which we know. In Jesus' name we pray. Amen.

4

EPHESIAN JEWS AND THE SPIRIT
ACTS 19

Review

Now we have discussed the question, "Does the Holy Spirit speak through a person when a person speaks in tongues?" And we decided that the Holy Spirit does not speak through a person, but a person himself speaks. Paul said, "if I pray in an unknown tongue, my spirit prayeth . . . " (I Cor. 14:14). And of course, this is consonant with I Corinthians 14, in which we have the gifts of the church set in order, particularly the gift of tongues. The abuse of the gift of tongues is corrected in I Corinthians 14. If the way the gift of tongues was used in the church was all of God, there would be no mistakes in the church. Nobody would have to correct anything, because God does not make any mistakes. Do you follow my thinking here? But man has a part in it and is to cooperate with God, and man can make mistakes and does make mistakes. That's why Paul had to correct the misuse of the gift of tongues in I Corinthians 14.

We had a very spiritual church where I was pastor. And if three messages were spoken in any one meeting, I would simply say to the folks, "God's been good to us, hasn't he? We've had three messages in tongues and interpretations. Let us have no more in this service. So that was the way we ran the church. That is scriptural. That is the way it ought to be.

Somebody said to me one time, "Yeah, but supposing God just moves on you for another one?" Well, God does not do it. That's all. It's that simple. "How do you know?" Because that's what the Word of God says. I Cor. 14:27, 28 tells us to let it be by two, or at the most by three, and that in turn. And then let someone interpret. And if there is no interpreter in church, even then let the person keep silence and speak to himself and to God. "Is that right?" Sure, it's right. And so if there's no interpreter, don't even talk in tongues in the church—that is, publicly, anyway.

Can one get a wrong experience? Is holiness a criterion? And why speak with tongues?

Now if you've been following along with me, you will have noted that this has been primarily a faith message—a message to build your faith, to believe that you can have what you want from God. And it works in the realm of the Holy Spirit also. If you want the Holy Spirit, you can have the Holy Spirit. If you, being evil, know how to give good gifts unto your children, how much more shall your heavenly Father give the Holy Spirit to them that ask him? But some of you have been asking a long time and still haven't got it. What happened? The Lord is still handing it out. So what happened? Well, you didn't know how to receive it. And in this series of messages, we're telling you how to receive it.

Somebody asked, "You mean you're going to tell us how to talk in tongues?" That's right, I will. Nobody else will, so I will. It makes me quite, quite unique, doesn't it? Don't miss the chapter, "After Tongues, What?" I want to tell you what's happened to some of the people who received in meetings, what they're doing for God. It's real. Believe me, it's real. One night after one service, a lady came up. She wanted to only hold her hands out and thought the power of God would just move down and come over and take control and make her talk in tongues. And she stood there really silently. So I said, "Okay, open your mouth and talk in tongues."

She began to cry, and she said, "I don't want to do it. I want Him to do it."

I said, "Honey, He ain't going to do it. So you have to do it." Then she opened her mouth and began talking in tongues.

But see, we have the wrong ideas. We've built them up over such a period of time. Really, I'm very bold in trying to undo in a book what you've learned over the last 30 years. That's a pretty big task, isn't it? But we're trying our best. Somehow, we think that God's just going to come down and do it. We want the supernatural so badly, yet we wouldn't want to do anything. We want to be sure it's real, and we don't know if it's real anyway. How do you know if it's real if you never had it? How are you going to measure it? How do you know? You don't. So you have got to take the word of somebody who is dealing with the subject and has practiced in the subject and knows what's going on. But I'll tell you one thing. If you'll keep it up, you'll find how real it is, because it will begin to work in your heart and your life and make something out of you. So it has been a faith message all the way.

Now let me say here. And I'm going to say it right now for those who would like to receive the baptism of the Holy Spirit. I don't hold up any criterion of holiness. I don't care what you're doing; I don't care how you're living. If you tell me you love Jesus Christ, you're invited to open your heart and receive the Holy Spirit. Now that's my statement. That's the way I feel about it. We've seen it work and we know what God does.

Some people want to wait until they get perfect to get the Holy Spirit. Of course, if you get perfect, you wouldn't need Him, would you? No, you wouldn't need Him if you got perfect. But Jesus offers the Holy Spirit for imperfect people. We're the ones that need Him. He takes us just as we are and fills us with the Holy Spirit.

Now let's bring you up to date. We discussed Matthew 3:11. John said, "I indeed baptize you with water unto repentance, but He that cometh after me is mightier than I, whose shoes I am not worthy to bear; He shall baptize you with the Holy Spirit and with fire." Jesus said in Acts 1:5, "Ye shall be baptized with the Holy Spirit not many days hence."

And then we saw that in Acts 10 the household of Cornelius received the Holy Spirit and the Church leaders called Peter on the carpet. Peter made the statement here in Acts 11:16, "Then remembered I the word of the Lord, how that He said, 'John indeed baptized with water but ye shall be baptized with the Holy Spirit.' " These three Scriptures all combine together to say one and the same thing. And we see that in the early New Testament church, every time they received the baptism of the Holy Spirit, they spoke in tongues. This is the way it is. This is the way it was then, and this is the way it is now.

When we say we are part and parcel of the early church, then we ought to have what the early church had. When you see the power the early church had, we ought to have the power the early church had. We ought to pray for the sick; we ought to preach the gospel; we ought to prophesy; we ought to testify; we ought to do just like the New Testament church did. If you travel in some of the circles I travel in, you hear statements like this: "Well, you know, the early church had to have these kind of things because people didn't know too much and couldn't read too much and weren't educated. So they had to do things like this to get the church started." I'm going to tell you, it got started in a blaze of glory and hasn't been the same since. If it is education that does this, the early church would have flopped. The vast amount of education that we have isn't doing what they did. And they didn't have half the education we have. Education doesn't save people. Don't misunderstand me. I've got education. I preach education. I say get all you can get. You need all you can get. But it doesn't save people. It takes the Spirit of God to save people and clean people up. We need what the early church had. So this is what we reiterate here.

Ephesian Jews Receive Baptism in the Spirit

Now in this chapter we're talking about the doctrine of the Holy Spirit. And we're looking into the account of the Ephesian Jews. Acts 19:1-7 states,

And it came to pass, that, while Apollos was at Corinth, Paul having passed through the upper coasts came to Ephesus: and finding certain disciples, he said unto them, 'Have ye received the Holy Spirit since ye believed?' And they said unto him, 'We have not so much as heard whether there be any Holy Spirit.' And he said unto them, 'Unto what then were you baptized?' And they said, 'Unto John's baptism.' Then said Paul, 'John verily baptized with the baptism of repentance, saying unto the people that they should believe on Him who should come after him, that is, on Christ Jesus. When they heard this, they were baptized in the name of the Lord Jesus. And when Paul had laid his hands upon them, the Holy Spirit came on them, and they spake with tongues, and prophesied. And all the men were about twelve.

May God bless this portion of his word to our hearts and minds.

Now many of us have read these Scriptures. And you have read it time and time again. Perhaps you have even used it to prove to the Baptists that they didn't have the Holy Spirit. You go and tell them all about it. In our churches most of us read so rapidly. We really skim the Scriptures. We don't really read sometimes. And we come up with some horrendous ideas sometimes, really, because we don't take time to see what it says. And here I'm going to look into it for you. I want you to examine it with me and let's see what really happened here.

We are very quick to settle for what seems to be the obvious answer. The obvious answers generally are not the right answers. The answers you have to dig for, generally, are the ones that are true after all is said and done. But we settle too easily and too quickly, and sometimes we don't have all the truth.

Number one, let me point out to you that when Paul came to Ephesus here, the people he met were not Christians. These were not Christians at all, not by any stretch of the imagination. These people were John's disciples. These were Jewish proselytes looking forward to a coming king, but not Christians resting on a finished redemption. How do we know this? Paul said they were baptized into John's baptism. That's the only baptism they had. We found out later on that Paul baptized them a second time in water, in Christian baptism, and made Christians out of them. So this group that Paul met was not Christian at all. Some people who don't know that say that when Paul met the Christians he asked these Christians, "Have ye received the Holy Spirit since ye believed?" But he wasn't talking to Christians. He was talking to disciples of John the Baptist.

Rhetorical Question

You cannot ask of a Christian, "Have you received the Holy Spirit since you believed?" We've already found out in Romans 8:9 that every Christian has the Holy Spirit. Romans 8:9 says, "if any man have not the Spirit of Christ, he is none of His." So you don't go around asking Christians "Have you received the Holy Spirit?" You're not sound if you do that. For anybody who knows anything knows that Christians have received the Holy Spirit. And the Apostle Paul was not that ignorant. He wrote most of the New Testament. He knew Christians had received the Holy Spirit. So he's not asking a stupid question here. Therefore, he's not talking to Christians. He's talking to the disciples of John the Baptist. The question, if addressed to Christians, is theologically untenable. It cannot be asked of a Christian.

The answer they gave to Paul was, "We have not so much as heard whether there be any Holy Spirit." Now that's not a correct answer any way you look at it. These are disciples of John the Baptist. Of course, they knew there was a Holy Spirit. John told them in Matthew 3:11, "I baptize you with water unto repentance. But He who comes after me is mightier than I. He shall baptize you with the Holy Spirit." They did know there was a Holy Spirit.

This is what I mean when I told you in the first place that it's not as easy as it sounds. Then what have we got here? How does it read? You have to look and see what we're talking about and what really is going on here.

We know they were not Christians because Paul said, "Unto what then were you baptized?" And again, a very interesting thing has occurred here, besides getting the truth out. I previously told you that something had to happen to give a New Testament preacher a reason to preach. And here was the reason to preach. He asked the question knowing they had not received, knowing he would get a negative answer. This gave him a reason to preach. And so he preached.

They received the message concerning Jesus Christ. Then Paul said, "John verily baptized with the baptism of repentance, saying unto the people, that they should believe on Him who should come after him, that is, on Christ Jesus. When they heard this, they were baptized in the name of the Lord Jesus." This is water baptism, a second baptism for them. Now this was Christian baptism. Then Paul laid his hands upon them, the Holy Spirit came on them, and they spoke with tongues and prophesied.

Now they were made Christians at this point. They became believers in Jesus Christ. Now let's go back and see what we have here. After giving it consideration and study, it appears to me that this question is purely a rhetorical question. Do you know what a rhetorical question is? Have you ever known somebody who you knew was not saved, but you wanted to testify to him? So you asked him if he was saved. And when he said "No," you had a chance to talk to him. Did you ever do that? That's what we call a rhetorical question. You were not expecting the right answer. You were expecting a wrong answer so you could talk to him. I think that's what Paul did here. "Have you received the Holy Spirit having believed?" "No." And he goes on and gets a chance to speak with them here.

The question is better phrased, "Have you received the Holy Spirit having believed?" Or, "Have you believed, and since then, received the Holy Spirit?" Now their answer was, "We have not heard that there is a Holy Spirit." This is not the best reading. A better reading is, "We have not heard that the Holy Spirit has been given." This makes more sense. And this is doctrinally correct and theologically correct. They did know there was a Holy Spirit, but they did not know that the Holy Spirit had been given. That makes sense, and that's really the answer that they gave. And again, the disciples' answer gave Paul a reason to preach the gospel. Consequently, he baptized them in water. This was Christian baptism. They are now believers. This is AD 54, some 21 years after Pentecost.

Now that's the way to understand the text in chapter 19. The obvious is not the answer. It's when you get into it and see what really took place that the truth comes out.

New Testament Pattern

Now we notice another thing here. This is the New Testament pattern. And for the life of me, I don't know why we don't do it today. But we don't. Somewhere in the very beginning, when people got saved, they got saved and filled with the Spirit and spoke with tongues all at the same time. Somewhere in the Church age, we've let this pattern drop off. Today, we get them saved, but we don't lead them into manifesting the baptism with the Holy Spirit. They should get it all at one time. And they could get it all at one time, if we'd communicate it to them. Many preachers are too easy and let them off the hook. Preachers today are so glad they got even one saved, that they're willing to give him a few days grace. Then they tackle him again, and hope they didn't lose him meanwhile. That's the way they're doing it now.

Method of Receiving

The Scripture says here that when the Ephesians heard this they were baptized in the name of the Lord Jesus. There is no waiting period, no grace period, no probation. They didn't have to become a church member, didn't have to sign a card. They didn't do anything! It says then that Paul laid his hands upon them, the Holy Spirit came on them, and they spoke with tongues and prophesied. Very simple! That's what they did. Paul immediately lays on hands to impart the Holy Spirit. This is the New Testament pattern, if you please. They speak in tongues and prophesy. No waiting! There was no tarrying.

We had the word *tarry* in Luke 24, and before Pentecost. But since Pentecost, the word *tarry* has never been brought up again. Nobody tarried since then to receive the Holy Spirit, because it's not a New Testament word. Not at all! And they didn't tarry in Acts 19. They didn't tarry here, because the Holy Spirit had already been given. The Holy Spirit had already been given because Jesus Christ had already been glorified. Since the day of Pentecost the Holy Spirit has been in the world. And He is present for every Christian to receive and to manifest.

However, we do have a little difficulty in our days that the apostles did not have. In those days, when the apostles went around preaching, whatever they said was considered true. Nobody in the Church contradicted them. And so when people got converted, they believed what the apostles said. They had what the apostles said they ought to have. It's not quite that simple now.

Today, there's no doubt that a person in America has already heard the gospel a lot of times. And finally he comes into your church and comes down and gets saved. But many new converts have also heard much for and against tongues, even before they get saved. Some of them even have their minds made up against tongues even before they get saved because of what they've already heard. So you can't get them in here, understanding the whole thing. They've already got their minds made up on that.

When I was with Raymond T. Richey years ago, he used to tell the sick before he would pray for them that they would have to be in his meetings for three nights. It would take three nights to get out of their heads what is wrong before he could get into their heads what is right.

And that's where we are today. We have the problem today. Before we can train people, we have to untrain them and get the wrong ideas out of their heads. Then we begin a period of retraining to get the right doctrine into their heads. That's our difficulty today, which the apostles didn't have in the early New Testament era.

Now we don't have the problem with people who don't know anything about it. I've been in the foreign fields many, many times where people know nothing. When you lay a hand on them, by the scores they just receive the Holy Spirit. They don't know anything against it, so they want everything God has for them! That's the condition that existed at Ephesus. I wish it existed in America, but it doesn't. We have to untrain them before we can get some training into them.

If people ask intellectual questions, you give intellectual answers. If they ask third grade questions, you give third grade answers. You can't give an answer greater than that they ask or they wouldn't understand you. Or if people ask stupid questions, you give stupid answers—the same level that they ask.

Now there is a third grade question or statement that goes around to which God gave me a beautiful third grade answer. Do you know what it is? Regarding Acts 8, somebody will say, "But it didn't say they spoke with tongues." And my third grade answer is, "No, and it did not say they didn't!" Now, that's pretty elementary. But it pretty well shuts them up, because that's the kind of question they asked and that's the kind of answer they receive. And then they don't know what to ask next.

But in Acts 19, they received the Holy Spirit and they spoke in tongues all at one time.

USS Coral Sea

I was on the USS *Coral Sea* in 1971-73. We had about one hundred sailors and officers receive the baptism in the Holy Spirit during my tour of duty in that carrier. God just nearly gave us the ship. We were an influence on that entire ship. I shall never forget one night in the ship's library, where the charismatic group met.

I'm telling you, we had a meeting. We had body ministry. We had everything going on down there. You name it, we had it! And if we didn't have it one night, we'd have it the next week, I'll tell you for sure. That's the way the Spirit was moving. And these fellows were fanning out through the ship, spreading the move of the Spirit everywhere they went.

Baptist Gunner's Mate Receives Baptism and Miraculous Healing

But I'll never forget one night. A Baptist gunner's mate slipped into the group. He didn't know why he came. But God knew. And he was sitting there with tattoos all up and down his arms. We were all talking in tongues and shouting the glory. And a couple of sailors prophesied and were singing in the Spirit. We were having a time. And I looked over at the gunner's mate and he didn't know what he'd got himself into. And so finally, I said, "Would you like to have us lay hands on you?" He shook his head. And so a couple of sailors and I went over and laid hands on that gunner's mate. And I mean the power of God hit that fellow. He jumped straight with his arms shaking and began to talk in tongues. And he knew nothing about the operation. Then he began to prophesy. I'm telling you, I thought the overhead was coming down that night. Now this fellow got the whole works at one shot. That's the way it's supposed to be.

Later on, at the close of the meeting, he said, "Let me testify." He said, "I didn't come down here to get this. But I got down here. When you asked me if I wanted you to lay on hands, the devil in me said 'No, don't do it.' But Jesus in me said, 'Yes, do it; it's right.' That's when I nodded my head." We laid hands on, and God filled him with the Holy Spirit.

But see, this is the way it is when the New Testament thing begins to work. A little later on, this gunner's mate had been working with some chemical acid and had burnt himself on the arm. It was a very severe spot, and it turned black. And one night we were down there, and some of the lads began praying for this gunner's mate. And all of a sudden he said, "Look." And before our very eyes that patch began to get smaller and smaller until it disappeared. God moved in a marvelous way. I've never seen anything like that in my life. But that happened to that gunner's mate on that ship. That makes believers out of people.

USS Galveston Sailor Gets Saved and Receives Baptism

I was the chaplain in the USS *Galveston*, one of our cruisers, some years ago. And we were off the coast of California. I got a letter from a sailor's mother. "Dear Chaplain, will you look up my son? He's a good boy, but he got into trouble." Was he in trouble! She didn't know what he was into. That was the understatement of the year. "He's a good boy." They're all good boys, you know, but they get in trouble. And so I thought, "Okay, I gotta write mother back," you know. So I got to see the guy. I found that he was a fireman down in one of the fire rooms. I called down there. I knew the petty officer, and he answered the phone. I said, "Hey, you got so and so down there, this is the chaplain."

"Yeah, Chaplain, what do you want?"

I said, "Well send him up. I gotta talk to him."

"Okay."

So he sent the sailor up. He was a tall, lanky sailor, and he walked up to my room. His little old white hat was over the back of his head, and you wouldn't think he had a care in the world. You'd think he owned the Navy. He'd had one court martial and was waiting for another one. Everybody was worried about it but him. He knocked and opened the door. I said, "Come in." He came in. I said, "Sit down." He sat down just as happy as he could be. The court martial didn't bother that lad. And I said, "You know why you're here?"

He said, "No."

I said, "Because your mother wrote me."

"Did she write you?"

I said, "Yeah, she wrote me." Sailors hate it when they write the chaplain. I said, "Yeah, you know why?"

"No."

"Because you won't write home. That's why she wrote me."

"Oh, she ought not to have done that."

And so I was getting ready to really give this sailor the business. I was going to really lay some words on him. Then I got to thinking that probably every officer he's got has already done that, including his petty officer, because he really loused up down in the fire room. And what happened, though, was the Lord got a hold of the chaplain's heart. And that was a miracle in itself. And all of a sudden I took a change of course. I smiled and said, "You know what?"

He said, "No, what?"
I said, "God loves you."

He said, "He does?"

I said, "Yeah, He does. Didn't you know that?"

He said, "No."

I said, "Well, He does. In fact, He loves you so much that Jesus Christ came and died on the cross so that you could be saved. Didn't you know that?"

He said, "No."

I said, "Well, He does." After sharing the Gospel, I said, "You know what?"

He said, "What?"

I said, "We could pray right here, and you could ask God to save you, and He would save you and forgive all your sins and take them all away. Did you know that?"

He said, "No."

I said, "Well, He would. Would you like to pray?"

He looked at me and said, "Yeah."

I said, "All right, bow your head." He bowed his head.

Then he said, "But wait a minute. I don't know how to pray."

I said, "I'll tell you what to say."

"Okay." So he bowed his head. I led that sailor in prayer, and he asked the Lord to save him and forgive him, and then I prayed for him. And I said, "Amen."

We both lifted our heads. He sat there for a couple of minutes. And then I got to thinking, "Why not go all the way." So I said, "You know what?"

He said, "What?"

I said, "You need the baptism in the Holy Ghost."

He said, "What's that?"

I said, "Let me show you."

This was so elementary, it's refreshing. I started with Acts 2. I read him the Scriptures. I said, "You notice these people, when they got filled with the Holy Ghost, they talked a language they never ever learned."

He said, "They did?"

I said, "Yeah, I just read it to you. Let me show you another one." I went to Acts 10 and said, "That's Cornelius, the centurion, you know? The military man? He spoke languages he never knew."

He said, "He did?"

I said, "Yeah, I just told you. I'll tell you what. Right now, we could bow our heads. I could lay my hands on you, and you could speak a language you never ever learned, if you received the Holy Spirit. Would you like to do that?"

He looked at me and said, "Yeah."

I said, "All right, bow your head." He bowed his head, and I laid my hand on that sailor's head. He raised both hands and began talking in tongues just like he knew what it was all about. Now this is the way it is. This is the way it was in the New Testament times. And then I let him go.

A few days later, I saw his petty officer. He said, "Hey, Chaplain, what in the world did you tell him?" I thought maybe he got in trouble again.

I said, "What's the matter? Is he getting along all right?"

He said, "Yeah, he's doing real good. What did you do to straighten him out? We couldn't straighten him out."

I said, "Well, he just got saved and filled with Holy Ghost."

He said, "Well I thought something happened."

And the next thing I heard was that he was after the petty officer to get him to go to church.

Well it is refreshing to see something work like this. But this is the way it ought to be. The only thing is, we have so many people on the outside who don't know what they're talking about. They muddy up the waters and get everybody confused. And the Baptists and Methodists and Presbyterians will screw it up. But they don't know what it's all about. That's the problem. If you ever get them straightened out, they will get filled with the Holy Spirit. And that's what we're trying to do, and we're also trying to get a few Pentecostal people squared away as we go too. If we can do that, it would be helpful.

Now this is the New Testament pattern and the New Testament way of operating, that people might be filled with the Holy Spirit. This is the way it works. And you don't have to be afraid to tell anybody what it's all about. In fact, tell them what it's all about. They're not going to know unless you tell them, are they? It is your job and my job to tell them what it's all about.

Practical Factors

Now let's get into some practical factors here. There are some of you who have not received the baptism of the Holy Spirit, spoken in tongues, or it's been years since you did. You need a refreshing. Why don't you get it while you're reading this book. Get it and stir it up. Stir up the gift that is within you.

Operating in the Flesh

Some people have a fear of getting in the flesh[5]. We in Pentecost have really been beat around the head and ears a long time. We've had people beat us up and down and say, "No, be careful." We're always so careful that we don't do anything! I'm tired of being careful! I'd rather strike out and do something wrong once in a while than be so careful, never to do anything. At least if you're doing something, God has a chance! And they say, "You gotta be careful you don't get in the flesh." Well, wait a minute! If you're not in the flesh, you won't need this anyway. You'd no longer be with us. Some people get those funny ideas.

Of course my answer to that is, "Go ahead! You've done everything else in the flesh. One more thing isn't going to hurt anyway!" That's right. Sure. We have done everything else in the flesh. It never bothered us. How come we get so pious now? But what happens is that we all get scared off. We're afraid to try anything. Then somebody says, "You've got to be careful of a wildfire." Honey, get some fire. Then we'll talk about wildfire. We haven't got enough fire to even worry about. Don't be scared of wildfire. You aren't going to run away with it! No!

But people think funny things. Some people say, "If I speak in tongues, it might be me." Well, of course. My answer is, "It won't be your mother." Of course it'll be you. And if it's not you, I want to get out of here fast.

My Spirit Prays

Now the Apostle Paul says, "if I pray in an unknown tongue, my spirit prayeth." It's my spirit that does the praying, not the Holy Spirit. It's me! It's me that does it. Now when I find out it's me that does it, then I can do it and quit when I want to, because I control my own spirit. And according to I Corinthians 14:32, the spirit of the prophet is subject to the prophet. And that principle holds for all who receive of the Spirit. We control ourselves. We control our own spirits.

The Holy Spirit Prompts

Acts 2:4, according to the Roman Catholic version, reads the best. It says, "They began to speak with other tongues as the Holy Spirit prompted them." He does the prompting but we do the speaking. If we would get ourselves under way and speak up and get in gear, He'll give us a language. But we have to get in operation.

The Flesh

Now concerning the flesh, listen to this. I suppose you prayed today. If you didn't, you ought to have. We all know we should. But how do you feel? Do you feel like you just always have got to pray every day, you just can't wait to pray? No, you don't feel that way. If you're like me, you go through a lot of scheduling conflict. But finally, you say to yourself, "Really, I must pray. I must pray. I know I should." I'll do everything in the world until I pray. So I make myself get down and pray! Do you do that? Sure you do. I don't feel like it, but I know I've got to, so I make myself start praying. I'm in the flesh! Pure and simple! But if I stay at it awhile, finally, I get in the Spirit. Then it begins to be a joy to pray, seek God, and be filled. But you start where you are even when you don't feel like it. But you start because you know you should. That's in the flesh.

Whenever you ever do something for God, you start in the flesh. But if you're going to do what God wants you to do, you eventually get in the Spirit, and God begins to move. So that's the way we start. If you're going to wait until you feel really religious, you'll never make it. Many of us never feel really religious.

Get a Start

Now you can make a start and speak in tongues, and the Spirit will eventually take over. I remember when I was at one naval air station, I had quite a heavy responsibility. I spent many days winding up being tired at the end of the day. I could go over to the little station chapel, go in there by myself, not feeling like it, but simply start speaking in tongues. I could kneel right in front of the altar and speak in tongues. It wouldn't be about five or six minutes, seemed like I'd feel a new energy come in my body. My mind would be refreshed. I'd feel all better again and get all prayed up, and get up and ready to go again, to do whatever God wanted me to do. You see, we're not dealing with a capricious God. There are laws that we can go by. If we understand them, we can work with them. We've got a constant source of energy and supply of the Spirit to help us and to keep us on the way. If you're going to always wait for the power to fall, honey, it won't fall. You've got to bring it on. There are some things we know to do, and that's why we're passing them on to you.

A Wrong Experience

Some people are afraid of getting a wrong experience or afraid they might get a wrong thing. I've heard people in olden days gone by say, "Well, you gotta be careful. You might get the wrong thing." Well, of course, if you've never had it, my first question is, How would you know if it's the wrong thing anyway? How do you know what you're looking for to be the wrong thing? How do you know that? How would you know if it's right or wrong? How do you know what to expect? How are you going to tell? All these questions have to be answered. However, listen. What kind of a God are we serving anyway? Do you mean to say if you come to the altar and seek to be filled with the Holy Spirit, you've got to keep one eye on God and be sure God gives you the right thing? Is that what you're saying? That is nearly blasphemy! One place I am safe is seeking God for the blessed Holy Spirit. If I seek Him for the Holy Spirit, that's what I'm going to get. "If ye then, being evil, know how to give good gifts unto your children, how much more shall your heavenly Father give the Holy Spirit to them that ask Him?" (Luke 11:13). If there's any place I'm safe, it's with the heavenly Father. I don't have to worry about a thing, what He's going to do, or what He's going to give me.

There is no such thing as getting a wrong experience. Misinformed good people have misinformed other good people and kept them from God's best. You're safe to come down and open yourself up to God and say, "God, give me all you've got. I want everything you've got for me!" And He'll give you what's right for you. He'll give the Holy Spirit. You don't have to be afraid of getting a wrong experience.

I had a person, whom I told to speak in tongues, come down one time and say to me, "Well yeah, but I don't know what to say." I said, "Of course not. If you did it wouldn't be tongues, would it?" As I previously said, someone couldn't remember the words he said the time before. You don't have to remember any words. And He doesn't want you to anyway.

Fears that Hinder Us

These kinds of questions are things that bother people. I have found out as I have traveled across the land and around the world that we Pentecostal people have fears that keep us from God. Yet, we're the ones who ought to know to be filled with the Lord, and filled with the Spirit. But we're the ones who are afraid! What are we afraid of? If you're afraid, then there's something wrong. Perfect love casts out fear. Of all people, we ought not have any fears or neuroses or psychoses. We ought to be sane and healthy-minded, filled with God and filled with goodness. That's what we ought to be. That's what the gospel of Jesus Christ does for us.

Some of us have let fears rob us of God's best. And if you have fears, then you're ignorant or not educated in the things of God.

But a little understanding of God's word can remove these fears and set you free. I've heard people say, "Yeah, but you've got to be careful, the devil speaks in tongues." I don't believe that, nor do I accept that at all. That's kept a lot of God's people scared and afraid. The devil doesn't speak in tongues. Neither does the Holy Spirit speak in tongues. We speak in tongues. Now we need to understand that. Somebody is always afraid.

Jesus said that a house divided against itself cannot stand (Mark 3:25). If the devil is divided against himself, he can't stand. So he's not going to talk in tongues. He doesn't do it. When you speak in tongues, God fills you, and you speak in tongues as the Holy Spirit prompts you.

Hypocrisy

I've heard people say, "Yes, but I'm afraid of being a hypocrite." You don't know what a hypocrite is if you make that kind of a statement. A hypocrite is someone who willingly tries to deceive somebody else, making himself something that he is not. If you're just a poor Christian trying to make it, and you're not doing too well, but you're honest, that does not make you a hypocrite! God will take you as you are, and give you the fullness of the Holy Spirit, and help you become the man or woman you ought to be. That doesn't make you a hypocrite. But we've let people scare us by saying, "Be careful, you might be a hypocrite." And we get scared of that. Why do you want to be afraid? After all, we're sinners saved by grace. That's the most you can say for any of us anyway, isn't it? We're only sinners saved by grace. If you admit that, you're no hypocrite. So go on and have what God's got for you. But the devil beats God's people over the head with this one.

Not Good Enough

Some people say, "But I'm not good enough to speak in tongues." No, of course, you're not. You're not good enough to get saved, but God saved you. You don't get anything by being good. If that was it, none of us would be here yet. None of us would be in the kingdom, because none of us are any good. There's none that are good, no not one! But we're here by God's grace. Because He called us, we're here. Like I said, the devil beats us over the head with some of these things.

Instructions to Receiving the Baptism

Now the days of tarrying are over. Now we have the laying on of hands. When hands are laid on you, your lips will begin to tremble. This is called stammering tongues in Isaiah 28:11. If at the moment hands are laid on you, you would go with it, you would not hinder it, you would not stop it, you would not make yourself speak in English or any acquired language, if you would open your mouth and just go with it, speak out anything you don't know, you'd be speaking in tongues in a matter of moments. It's so simple, you would think you're doing it all by yourself. It's that simple.

Somebody might say, "You going to tell us what to say?" Sure. Or he might say, "But I don't want to imitate anybody." The Apostle Paul says, "Imitate me as I imitate Christ." That's a good principle. But the Church hears so many off-hand statements, that it doesn't know what to think sometimes. We need to get back to the Scriptures. Now if listening to me or anybody else speak in tongues will liberate you and make you free to speak in tongues, then do it. God will then set you free to speak in tongues as you wish. This is the way it is. You've got to use your mouth, your vocal cords, your breath, and your lips. You've got to use it yourself, and if you'll put it into operation, then the language will come, and you will be filled with the Holy Spirit. This is the way it is. This is the way we've seen it happen. And so God will fill you, too.

Benediction

Heavenly Father, we're thankful for your goodness to us, and your mercies. God, bless these people. Fill thy people with the Holy Spirit. Those who've let the gift lie dormant, Lord, stir the gift that is within them, that they get a refreshing. Amen.

5

THE REVIVAL AT SAMARIA
ACTS 8

Review

We discussed the question, "Does the Holy Spirit speak through a person when he speaks in tongues?" We've decided that He does not. A person speaks in tongues himself. It's his own spirit doing the praying.

We also discussed the question, "Can one get a wrong experience when he seeks the Holy Spirit and speaks in tongues?" And we decided that he could not. Anybody who comes to God to get the Holy Spirit is going to get the Holy Spirit. That's all there is to it—no two ways about it. You don't have to worry about what God's going to do. You don't have to keep an eye on Him. You're safe in the house of God. Any time you want to seek God, you'll always get the right thing. Now aren't you glad to know that? Sure you are.

Introduction

If you've been taking notes, you will remember that in Matthew 3:11, John said, "I indeed baptize you with water unto repentance; but He that cometh after me is mightier than I, whose shoes I am not worthy to bear. He shall baptize you with the Holy Spirit, and with fire." We have a similar statement given in John 1:33, where John says, "And I knew Him not, but He that sent me to baptize with water, the same said unto me, 'Upon whom thou shalt see the Spirit descending, and remaining on Him, the same is He which baptizeth with the Holy Spirit.'" And then we brought to your attention Acts 1:5, where Jesus said, "ye shall be baptized with the Holy Spirit not many days hence," or not many days from now. And then in Acts 2:4, we had the event in which they were filled with the Holy Spirit. And in Acts 11:16, Peter was called on the carpet at Jerusalem after he preached at Cornelius's house where Cornelius and his household received the Holy Spirit. He said, "Then remembered I the word of the Lord, how that He said, John indeed baptized with water, but ye shall be baptized with the Holy Spirit."

He called the occasion at Cornelius's house at Caesarea the baptism in the Holy Spirit. If you compare Matthew 3:11, Acts 1:5, and Acts 11:16, the term is called, *the baptism in the Holy Spirit*. And we saw that at Cornelius's house the phenomenon of tongues occurred. And in Ephesus when Paul came through and met John's disciples, as we discussed in chapter 4, he laid hands on them, and they received the Holy Spirit, and the evidence of tongues was there. So it seems to me it just doesn't take a lot of brains to understand this. It just seems like, if you're logical in your thinking, it's a natural conclusion to come to, that this is in name and terminology *the baptism in the Holy Spirit*.

Now we're going to move on a bit further. We're going to read Chapter 8 of Acts and discuss the revival in Samaria. We're also going to discuss the tongues situation in Samaria. We are discussing this situation after the others since this is most peculiar. And this study will wind up the doctrinal phase of the baptism in the Holy Spirit. By now, you should pretty well understand what the baptism in the Holy Spirit is.

The Revival at Samaria

Now in Chapter 8 of Acts, concerning Stephen,

Saul was consenting unto his death. And at that time there was a great persecution against the church which was at Jerusalem. And they were all scattered abroad throughout the regions of Judea and Samaria, except the apostles. And devout men carried Stephen to his burial, and made great lamentation over him. As for Saul, he made havoc of the church, entering into every house, and haling men and women, committed them to prison. Therefore they that were scattered abroad went everywhere preaching the word. Then Philip went down to the city of Samaria, and preached Christ unto them. And the people with one accord gave heed to those things which Philip spake, hearing and seeing the miracles which he did. For unclean spirits, crying with loud voice, came out of many that were possessed with them, and many taken with palsies, and that were lame, were healed. And there was great joy in that city (Acts 8:1-8).

Verses 14-17 say, "Now when the apostles who were at Jerusalem heard that Samaria had received the word of God, they sent unto them Peter and John, who, when they were come down, prayed for them, that they might receive the Holy Spirit. For as yet He was fallen upon none of them; only they were baptized in the name of the Lord Jesus. Then laid they their hands on them, and they received the Holy Spirit."

Downfall of American Empire

Now for a bit I want to discuss this subject of Holy Spirit revival, which certainly is a need in our land today. I don't have to go into details, and I shall not need to in order to tell you that we are in desperate straits in America today. We're living in trying times. And ladies and gentlemen, it's not going to all be easy. We may have a downfall of our empire in our day. That's a possibility. And we're morally decadent. We're morally in trouble. And it seems like the American people can't get a hold of themselves. We must have Holy Spirit revival today to save our nation and to save our generation. No less will do. The fact that we've had revival in times past will not do for today. Every generation has to have revival and every generation has to save its generation. You can't reach back. Time goes on too speedily.

Formality will not do. Church programming will not do. It will take real Holy Spirit spirituality. Now don't misunderstand me. Being a Navy chaplain, I am well acquainted with liturgy. I am well acquainted with formality in services. And I know enough to appreciate it. I think there's room for it. What I am saying is, the formality alone will not save nor keep us from falling. And we need to understand this.

In Holy Spirit revival there is seen the moving of the Holy Spirit, the outpouring of the Spirit, the manifestations of the Spirit, the gifts of the Spirit, and healing. And all this goes on with Holy Spirit revival. When the Holy Spirit begins to move over a locality or a community, or over the land, there is seen the supernatural, and that's what makes our religion so enjoyable. I would hate to be in some church where you never enjoyed your religion, like some people are. Their religion is a hum-drum thing. It's a boring thing. They go, but they don't know why. They don't get any joy out of it. I'd hate to belong to a religion like that, wouldn't you?

But when God begins to move, and the Holy Spirit begins to sweep over us, then He puts joy in our hearts. He puts a song in our hearts. He fills our hearts with the Holy Spirit, and it makes our salvation enjoyable as we move along here below. And this is what separates us from the denominational bodies, really. The fact is that we enjoy the moving of the Holy Spirit, and God comes down and takes control and lifts us up out of the hum drum of everyday life and gives us a touch of heaven and forgives our sins, puts lightness in our hearts again, and sends us on our way.

We must be filled with the Spirit if we're to have true Holy Spirit revival. The need is clear—to stem the tide of immorality on one hand and to save souls on the other. I don't need to go into detail to tell you that education doesn't save souls, though we need it—all of it we can get. But it takes a genuine moving of the

Holy Spirit to bring men and women, boys and girls, to conviction wherein they will forsake and confess their sin and ask God to save them and to deliver them. This is the work of the Holy Spirit.

Method of Reception

Now let's notice the order of events in the Samaritan revival. Somehow it seems to me that we can have what happened in the New Testament since we're part of the New Testament church. We can have revival too, if we're willing to pay the price and actually desire it. Charles Gunderson Finney in his day laid out some concepts and precepts for having revivals. And I'm inclined to believe he's right. It takes sacrifice on the part of God's people if we're going to have a revival. There's got to be real prayer. There's got to be real desire. There's got to be a real burden. There's got to be all of this, if we're going to have real revival.

In our day and time it seems to me like we have been getting softer by the year until when we talk sacrifice today, nobody even understands what we're talking about. You talk about getting under the burden today. But people don't seem to understand what that is. Some of you old-timers know what I'm talking about when I talk about paying the price, getting under the burden, and all of this. But friends, if we're going to have revival, that's what it's going to take. Let's see what happens here in Samaria.

Scattered and Persecuted Church

Now as we look into the Scriptures in this chapter, we see that what happened was that the revival in Samaria was all centered around the fact of the scattering of the church when Saul of Tarsus set out to wreck it. Now one thing you can say about Saul is that he had a mind. And brother, when Saul made up his mind to do something, he pretty well did it. He had his mind made up to wreck the church. And I suppose he would have done it had not Jesus reached down and saved him. Christ had to save Paul to save the Church, because Paul was going to tie it up. He had his mind made up to it, and he was a powerful character. But you know the story, how God reached down and saved Paul, appeared to him on the Damascus road, filled him with the Holy Spirit, and turned him around later on and made him one of the chief apostles.

But this revival had to do with the persecution. The people were scattered throughout all the region. As they were scattered, they went everywhere preaching the word. One thing about these people, as far as we can ascertain, is that there was no complaining to them. Nobody said, "Oh I had to give up my home or my house, or whatever I had." We have none of that here. It seems like when they were scattered, they all went preaching the Word. They all took the gospel of Jesus Christ on their lips.

I've heard people in our day and time, and I'm sure you have too, who maybe had to give up something to serve the Lord. But they're quick to let you know what they had to give up to serve Jesus. My friends, when I hear people talking like that, it makes me feel they're sorry they did it. If you're sorry you had to give up for something, you really didn't give up very much after all. And for the life of me, I can't see where most of us have sacrificed, hardly at all anyway.

I've been in the naval service for 28 years, and I've heard people say they've had to be gone from home. They say that's sacrifice. I guess it is, but it's never entered my head that that's sacrifice. I counted it such a privilege that God had called me to preach the gospel. The fact I can preach it where I am, to me, has been a blessing to me, as well as to the other people who get saved. I don't count it as sacrifice. I don't think many of us have been in the place of real sacrifice really. So we can't really say much about it.

But they went, gave up all they had, being persecuted, scattered throughout the regions of Samaria, and they preached the gospel of Jesus Christ. They had power in their lives! And they had victory in their lives! No wonder when they got to Samaria there was a great revival that took place down there!

New Testament Pattern

The Scripture says, "Philip preached Christ unto them" (Acts 8:5). Now that's a New Testament pattern also. Every time these people got an opportunity to preach, they preached the Lord Jesus Christ—the fact that He lived and died and rose again. The rising again was always the main part of it. The fact that He still lives to make intersession for His people was the story that they took with them. They preached Christ unto them.

Results

Now notice in the revival here, miracles are wrought. The lame are walking, the blind see, the palsies were healed, and demons are being cast out. That's a great sign of revival. But that is not just for the people like Philip. It's for all of God's people! For we see in Mark 16, where Jesus says, "Go ye into all the world, and preach the gospel to every creature. He that believeth and is baptized shall be saved; but he that believeth not shall be damned. And these signs shall follow them that believe: In my name shall they cast out devils; they shall speak with new tongues; they shall take up serpents; and if they drink any deadly thing, it shall not hurt them; they shall lay hands on the sick, and they shall recover" (vv. 15 – 18). That's what Jesus said about His own people. None of them have to be ordained ministers. They don't have to be deacons in the church. They can be anybody who will believe God for great and mighty things, and God will use them for His own glory in the church. That's what it says!

Oh, it seems to me sometimes we have fallen below our privilege! We're not living up to what Christ wants us to have! But worse yet, we're willing to settle for less. And that's what makes it so bad. We need to say, "God give us revival; God start in my heart, and bring us back to New Testament Christianity where we see these things take place."

Great Commission in Acts

Now the power of the Spirit is seen at work. Well, Jesus said, "Ye shall receive power, after that the Holy Spirit is come upon you, and ye shall be witnesses unto me both in Jerusalem, and in all Judea, and in Samaria, and unto the uttermost part of the earth" (Acts 1:8). In Acts chapters one through seven, Judea is evangelized. From Acts eight to the middle of Acts, Samaria is evangelized. In the last half of Acts the outermost parts of the earth is evangelized. And so the whole promise is fulfilled, just like it was given when Jesus spoke it. The power of the Spirit is seen at work. The word is believed.

So in this context the Samaritans received Christ. If you know who the Samaritans were, you would know they were a half-breed Jew from many generations back. They were despised by the Jews and despised by the Gentiles, because they were half-breeds. Nobody was for them at all. But here, a great revival occurred in Samaria. The Samaritans not only believed, they repented, they received Christ, and then they were baptized in water! Now in the New Testament church, when people were baptized in water, you could pretty well count on it that they had been saved, because the early church did not baptize anybody unless they were thought to be saved. And so the Samaritans here were baptized in water. I think one of the greatest statements in the New Testament is found in Acts 8:8 where Luke says, "There was great joy in that city." That's an understatement.

Demonized Teenager Delivered

I shall never forget an event some years ago. I was a member of the Southern California District of the Assemblies of God. And we had our annual district council in Pasadena at the Shakespeare Auditorium. And I tell you the whole story, as we know it developed. But Dr. Cecil Lowry was the speaker on that occasion. In the night service Dr. Lowry had preached. That night, sitting on the back pew was a back-slidden Pentecostal father and his son. Now this boy was just 17 years of age. He was a stripling of a lad, just a small-framed boy. Yet he was very violent. He would swear at his dad and tell his dad off. And worse than that, he would slap his mother around, and his father would permit it. That's one thing I've never understood, but he did.

Anyway, that night, they sat there and the altar call was given. And the boy said to his father, "Give me the keys; I'm going to go sit out in the car and wait for you there."

And for once his father had the strength to tell him something. He said, "You sit right here 'til this is over."

Well, in a few moments, the two got up and went forward to the altar. And when they got down there, everything went all right for a while until the brethren laid hands on this boy. And when they laid hands on him, a demon took possession of him. The small lad picked up a folding chair and he brought it down over his head and broke that thing to smithereens. He had assumed superhuman strength in that very short time.

Well, of course, you know in a public service you can't have this going on. We had so many visitors there. It took twelve strong men to get hold of that lad and finally get him back behind the stage where we could pray with him. This kid was violent! My, what superhuman strength he had. They got him back to a room. I joined the group back there as they went to pray for this boy. And so one of the ministers said, "Don't you know you're going to hell?"

And the lad said, "Yes." He was lying on a couch there.

The minister said, "Do you want to go to hell?"

And the lad said, "Yes."

Now that is not the mind of a rational 17-year-old boy. And so we prayed and we prayed. Well, it got to be midnight and the custodian wanted to close the building. So he asked us, "Could you take the lad somewhere else?" Well, we took him over to Trinity Assembly of God and we continued praying with the lad. We had

him in a prayer room, lying on a couch. Two-thirty a.m. came
about. All of a sudden, the lad slipped off the couch, on his knees,
and onto the floor, and began to pray and asked God to save him.
He asked Jesus to come into his heart. And after that, he stood up.

Now he's normal. He's in his right mind. I always thought
people should testify when they can. And so I remembered how
he treated his mother. We were all standing up now. So I asked the
lad, "Would you like to testify?" Now he was not the violent lad.
He was the meek 17-year-old boy now. He said, "No, I want to go
tell Mom." I thought of verse 8, "There was joy...." I bet there was
joy in that home that night when this boy told momma that he'd
got straightened out and Christ came into his life. There was joy!
Christ does bring joy! Lives are straightened out, and minds are
set straight when people receive the Lord Jesus Christ.

Healing of the Injured Machinist and the Presbyterian Lady

I'll never forget, some years ago, I was pastor of a church in
the San Diego area. And the Lord had lit on my heart to preach
through the Book of Acts in one year. And so this particular Sunday
morning, I was to preach on the third chapter of Acts regarding
the story of the healing of the man at the Beautiful Gate. And I'd
done all the preparation. I was putting on the finishing touches
with my typewriter that evening before going to bed. And I'm not
given to hearing voices or anything of this nature. I'm not psychic.
I don't claim to be at all. But as I was sitting at the typewriter, I
thought I heard a voice say to me, about the healing of the man at
the Beautiful Gate, "I'll do that for you in the morning." It so shook
me up. I looked around, and not a soul was there. I was by myself!
Yet, I heard the voice say that! Then, of course, I couldn't think of
anybody in the church who was sick like this you know. And so it
dearly worried me. But I went to bed.

The next morning was Sunday morning. We got up and went
to church. Of course, by this time I had the business of the Sunday
School and the church services. I forgot all about the experience of
the night before. And that morning, a man came into the church

just bent double. I said, "What's the matter with you?" Well, he was a machinist. He had injured his back. Unthinkingly, I just said, "Well God will heal you this morning." And so the service came and went, and God did bless in a wonderful way. We had a good meeting. The Spirit of God was poured out, and we gave an invitation for healing that morning. Quite a number of people came and filled the whole front row of the big tabernacle down there.

The first lady I prayed for I always called a Presbyterian. I don't know what she was. She was not a member of the church, but she came all the time. She was very quiet. She was sitting over to the left side. And so I went down to her, and I said, "What's the trouble, sister?"

She said, "Well, something is wrong with my leg." She could hardly walk.

I said, "Will you come with me?"

She said, "Yes."

I grabbed her by the hand, and I jerked her out of that pew. I'm telling you it's a good thing she did walk. If she hadn't, she'd have fallen. But she did. She straightened right up and began to walk. God had touched her right there.

And on down it went 'til I got to the man who had been bent double. We had opera chairs in the church—arms on them. And so, by the time I got to this man, he was leaning on the arms of the chair, trying to get up by the time I got there. By the time I got there, I simply put my hand in the middle of his back and I shoved as hard as I could shove. I said, "In the name of Jesus, walk!" Again, had he not walked, he would have fallen flat on his face, and I would have been the biggest fool in town that day. But he walked. He straightened up immediately and threw his hands up and began to praise God. God had touched him.

Then I remembered the night before, how God said, "I'll do that for you in the morning." This is what happens when God begins to move and faith begins to run high and people begin to believe God for things! This is Holy Ghost revival, if you please. God moves in a wonderful way.

Back to Samaria

So Samaria received the Word of God. When the Scriptures say that anybody received the Word of God, that's tantamount to saying, "They received Christ." They've become believers. That terminology means the same thing.

Furthermore, the Samaritans received the baptism of the Holy Spirit. Now it says in verses 14 - 17, "Now when the apostles which were at Jerusalem heard that Samaria had received the word of God, they sent unto them Peter and John, who, when they were come down, prayed for them, that they might receive the Holy Spirit. For as yet He was fallen upon none of them; only they were baptized in the name of the Lord Jesus. Then laid they their hands on them, and they received the Holy Spirit."

Now this is a problem area. And like I say, and I think I told you in the last chapter, we don't read very critically. We'll settle for anything. Most of us will. But this is a very critical passage. If you've been reading critically in the last few chapters and understanding what I've had to say, you will realize how critical this is.

All Believers Have the Spirit

In the first place, you've got a group of saved, baptized believers. And according to our text here, it says they had not received the Holy Spirit. Now this is theologically untenable! For we've already seen in Romans 8:9 that "if any man have not the Spirit of Christ, he is none of His." Yet these people have the Spirit of Christ; they have received Christ into their lives, and they've been baptized in water. Well, what are we talking about then? Ah, that's what I want to tell you, and that's what you're reading this chapter to find out.

Confusion in Terms

I will share a better thought here. Here we have the fact that the people had been saved and received Christ. I will share a better reading here. There are two different terms that are used in the Greek text. When we see the word *receive* in the King James Version, it doesn't really tell the whole story just like it is.

Now let me put it to you this way. When a person gets saved, he receives the Spirit into his heart. The Greek text uses the word *dexomai,* to receive into one's person. They received the Holy Spirit, and so are saved. Now this is true with all believers.

When it talks about receiving the Holy Spirit, there is another word used, the Greek word *lambano,* which carries this idea: to receive into manifestation or manifesting the Holy Spirit. It is a different thought altogether. In the King James Version, the only word used is *received,* and you cannot pick up the difference or the shade of meaning. But if you understand it this way, you would understand that the Samaritans got saved, received Christ, they received the Holy Spirit into their own souls—into their hearts. Yet they're going to receive the Holy Spirit in manifestation when the apostles lay hands on them. Have I made it clear? I hope I have.

So the reception of the Holy Spirit mentioned here has to do with the manifesting of the Holy Spirit and not the initial reception into one's own heart and mind. Now that's the difference. And if you think of it this way, then the Scriptures are tenable. They're in line, they're congruous, and no problem exists. But if you don't think that, you've got a problem you can't answer. And this is one of the greatest problems to the denominations today. They can't understand this for some reason, and I don't know why. They all go to college but they don't seem to pick this up. Of course they don't teach this in colleges, either. You have to kind of dig it out for yourself. But those of us who are earnest and sincere have got to come up with answers. And so this is what we do. We go to the text, and we find out what happened. And this is what happened.

Now the apostles heard that Samaria received the Word of God. That is, they got saved. Not only that, but they got baptized with water. And the apostles at Jerusalem knew this. And the apostles or the church, the mother church at Jerusalem, is not content to leave the Samaritans just like they are, without the manifestation of the Holy Spirit. They're not content for this at all, because they realize the Samaritans need power for service. They need power for victorious living. They need power to do something for God. They need power in prayer. The apostles knew this, and they were not going to leave them alone without it. It's an amazing thing.

R.A. Torrey

R.A. Torrey, the great Baptist Bible scholar, made this statement. He says that in the early church, when one group of Christians found another group of Christians, the first question they would ask was, "Have you received the Holy Spirit?" If the answer was that they had not, the first group immediately saw to it that they did.

I've often wondered what would happen if I would say, "Now, tonight, we're going to lay hands on everybody to get the baptism of the Holy Spirit, and you won't be allowed to go home 'til you get it," Everybody would say, "Oh, yeah? You and who else is going to make me?" But you would think that Christians would want to be filled, that they would want somebody to help them, and that they would want all that God has for them, wouldn't you? And so the early church knew that the Samaritans needed to manifest the Holy Spirit. And don't miss the next chapter. I'm going to tell you the value of manifesting the Holy Spirit. You need to know this.

And so the apostles were sent down. Now you see another thing. When they sent the apostles down, we find out what the work of an apostle is. The work of an apostle is to impart the Holy Spirit. That's his job. And that's why they sent them down here.

Gifts of the Spirit

Now we notice the work of the minister here. Everybody knows his place. Let me bring this to your attention. Philip was a deacon. That's all he was. He was not a minister. He was neither licensed nor ordained. He was a deacon. But I'll say one thing. He certainly knew how to "deac." He knew that much. He was used of God in a mighty way. But let me say this. The apostles were no better men than was Philip. They were not more spiritual than Philip, not at all. Philip was not inferior to the apostles. Not at all. Neither was he greater than the apostles. Not at all. We're so quick to judge ourselves by one another. He does this. Even I do that. We really ought not do that. We ought not compare ourselves with anybody. If you want to compare yourself, compare yourself with what you are and what you want to be. That's the way to compare yourself.

But the church sent Peter and John down to pray for them. Each one knew his place. Philip was the evangelist. He knew his gifts. He knew his ministry. And he knew his limitations. He knew what God would have him do, and allow him to do. He knew that. And the apostles had their job to do—that was to impart the Holy Spirit. I've often thought of it this way. I don't know that this happened, but I've often thought of it like this. When Peter and John arrived down there, I think there was the utmost of courtesy. I think there was ministerial courtesy and ethics on all hands. I think that when Peter and John saw Philip, they said, "God bless you, man. You've done a wonderful piece of work down here. This is outstanding. We're glad to come down here and be helpful to you."

I think Philip probably said, "Brethren, I'm glad you've come. We've done what we could. God has been good to us. Come on and impart the Spirit to these people so they can go ahead and speak in tongues." I think they just worked together like that—no jealousy, no quibbling about anything, everybody working together and pulling in the same fashion.

Friends, I'm going to tell you something. If we Pentecostal people could ever get our heads together and get our hearts together, and put our shoulders to the plow, and move in one direction, we could move the world for God. But so many times we want to pull in another direction.

Illustration

I saw a cartoon the other day. Of course, it was about the President. The cartoon showed two figures on a bicycle, faced in opposite directions. One bicycle with two seats faced in opposite directions. They were both pedaling to go in opposite directions. Sometimes I think that's the way it is with our churches. We're all pedaling, but in different directions. If we could ever get on the same way, we'd make it.

I saw another cartoon. This is supposed to be true. It showed two other men on another bicycle with two seats facing forward. The first man had no body from the waist on down. But he had arms. He was sitting on the front bicycle seat steering. The man behind him had no arms. So he was doing the pedaling. They were going somewhere. They both got together.

If we in the church could ever get going in the same direction, pooling our resources, putting our heads together, putting our minds together, giving it all we had, there's no telling what we could do. God help us to get ourselves together and go in the right direction. So no jealousy, perfect harmony, everybody preferring one above the other, and that's what happened with the apostles and Philip in Samaria.

Manifest, Not Receive

Now the apostles prayed for them that they might receive the Holy Spirit. Again I bring to your attention that this word *receive* can be replaced with *manifest*,[6] so that verse 15 could read. "they prayed for them that they might manifest the Holy Spirit." That's a good term here, because they had already received the Holy Spirit into their hearts. They were not going to receive another outside Spirit. God was not going to come into them in a different way.

They had already received Christ, but what they had was going to be manifested when the apostles laid hands on them. This was what was going to happen. And those of you who've been in the meetings, you've been finding out that all we've had to say in all these meetings is that there is nothing from outside coming in at all. It's what you had from within that's going to manifest itself outward. That's the baptism in the Holy Spirit, or the manifestation of the Spirit.

Two Methods of Receiving: Sovereign Will of God and Laying on of Hands

So the apostles prayed for them. There was no rush act, no foolishness, no silliness. And the Samaritans prayed also. There were no shortcuts. It's amazing how many people want shortcuts today. Honey, there're not any shortcuts. But there're God's ways, God's way of doing it. And you don't have to tarry. That's not a New Testament thing. If you want to call out a shortcut, call out one if you want to. That's just God's way. That's all. God has two ways of filling people today. One is in a sovereign method in which the Holy Spirit just moves. Another is when somebody like me or others just come around and lay on hands. God moves in both ways.

Prerequisites

The prerequisites are that hearts must be right with God. That has to do with the thoughts or motives. That does not mean the individual has to be perfect. If it meant that people had to be perfect, then nobody could get it, because nobody is perfect. And if you were perfect, you wouldn't need it then. So we're not talking about perfection. We're talking about this thing of motive, and that's the thing we're concerned with--making restitution, making things right with God, making things right with men! And then the apostles laid hands on them. This is quite in order.

And I believe that instructions preceded the laying on of hands. I do not believe we can come into a meeting cold and just lay on hands and people receive the Holy Spirit. It won't work that way.

I believe in the New Testament church; I think they got together and had prayer. They talked about the Word of God. They told the people what to expect, how to cooperate with God. Then when they laid hands on them, people received the Holy Spirit. I believe that's the way they did. And that's what we've seen in our meetings across the land and literally around the world.

Now another thing! The candidates must believe and obey the apostles. I've been in meetings where people didn't want to do what I told them to do. If you don't want to do what I tell you to do, you remove yourself from my ability to help. I can't help you. But if you'll do what the man of God says to do, you'll have what the man of God says you ought to have. It's that simple. That's the way it is. And that's the way it will be.

Evidence of Tongues in Acts 8

Some of the denominational people will say, "Well Acts 2, 10, and 19 say they spoke with tongues. But what about Chapter 8? It doesn't say they spoke with tongues. And like I said, God gave me a third grade answer to that third grade statement. And that simply is this, "No, but it didn't say they didn't." You know, as I told you in the last chapter, you've got to answer people's questions on the level they ask them. If they ask you an intellectual question, you give an intellectual answer. If they ask you a stupid question, you give a stupid answer—on the same model. They understand it that way. And when I answer them with that one, that seems to satisfy them perfectly. And then they don't know what happened.

All right now! Concerning the text in Acts 8, we have some statements made here by the great divines of days gone by from various denominations concerning the Samaritans.

Matthew Henry, the great scholar, says, "They were endued[4] with the gift of tongues which seems then to have been the most usual, immediate effect of the pouring out of the spirit. This was both an imminent sign to them that believed not, and of excellent service to them that did."

Adam Clark, the noted Methodist commentator, says, "It was the miraculous gifts of the Spirit which were thus communicated, the speaking with different tongues and these extraordinary qualifications which were necessary for the successful preaching of the gospel."

Joseph Benson, another Methodist, says, "These new converts spoke with tongues and performed other extraordinary works."

Charles John Ellicott, an Episcopalian, says, " 'When Simon saw that through the laying on of hands,' these words imply that the result was something visible and conspicuous. A change was wrought and men spoke with tongues and prophesied."

D.D. Wheaton says, "It's a miniature Pentecost, the same charismatic effusions."

Alexander McClarendon, the noted Baptist, says, "The Samaritans had been baptized but still they lacked the gift of the Spirit until this time of the laying on of hands."

And J.S. Excel, who is the co-editor of the *Pulpit Commentary*, says, "This shows that the recipients of the Holy Spirit must in some external fashion, probably through speaking with tongues or working miracles, have indicated their possession of the heavenly gift."

Now that's what these great divines said. And, of course, I must remind you of this. Any time you discuss the New Testament, any of the New Testament, every writer in the New Testament was a person who spoke with tongues. And every one of them wrote to people who spoke with tongues. If you don't believe it, then to that group you're not even on the inside track! That's the context in which the whole thing takes place. Now, if we understand, it helps a little, doesn't it? All right!

Gayle Jackson

Some years ago, while I was pastoring in the San Diego area, Gayle Jackson came. Now I don't know if Gayle had ever been in this area or not. But Gayle Jackson came to San Diego to First Assembly for a city-wide meeting. We who had churches out on the outskirts of town all cooperated with the big church to be included in that big meeting. And so the last three nights of the meeting, Gayle Jackson preached on the baptism of the Holy Spirit. Talk about preaching, brother, that man was a preacher.

He would preach three nights. Those that wanted to receive the Holy Spirit had to be in the meeting three nights. And then on the third night, the ministry team would lay on hands for them to receive. Now they had to have a ticket to get in. It didn't cost anything. But the church was crowded. So everybody who wanted to receive the Holy Ghost had to have a ticket to get in to get a place to sit down. And so that night, just before the last night, before we laid on hands, Jackson met with the ministry team. He said, "Now, to let the people know that this is not my doing, and you people have not preached, you will go out to the congregation and lay on hands." I thought that was wonderful. I've always believed in this anyway, you know. One of the ministers said to me, "What do you think about that, Linzey?" I said, "Well it's in the Bible isn't it?" Well he was no longer a friend of mine after that, because he wanted to find fault.

And so after Jackson talked with us, we went up into the auditorium. Then another person, who was a friend of mine, went up on the platform with his fingers crossed. He didn't believe it would work! I thought, "My Lord, where are we? If we in the ministry can't believe, what's going to happen?" So we got up there. And a full house! A Baptist minister friend of mine who wanted to receive walked into the back door. He waved his card. He wanted me to see it. So I waved back to him. He was going to get the Holy Spirit. And a professor friend of mine from the Baptist seminary sat in the balcony with his horned-rimmed glasses on. He wasn't going to miss a thing. And I'm telling you, we had a meeting that night.

And so after Jackson preached, then we of the ministry team fanned out through the auditorium. Then came up one little elderly lady. I said, "Sister, would you receive the Holy Spirit if I lay on hands?"

She said, "I would."

I laid hands on her; she just raised her head and began talking in tongues. It followed like that. So I moved on down the row and met a man. He looked like a carpenter, a well built individual—a middle-aged man. I said, "Sir, would you receive the Holy Spirit?"

He said, "Yes."

I laid hands on him; he raised his hands and began talking in tongues just like that. Easy!

And then I got down to the front a few moments later. The Baptist preacher came over and said, "I got it, I got it! But my wife hasn't got it. "Will you pray for her?"

I said, "Where is she?"

"Well, she's down by the pillar, praying.

I went down and laid hands on her head and I said, "Sister, receive the Holy Spirit."

She raised her hands and she began talking in tongues. I'm telling you, we had a time that night. Actually, I think 120 received the baptism in the Holy Spirit that night, in the church at San Diego.

That's the way God moves. When the Spirit begins to move, God begins to do something, hearts begin to get touched, and hearts open themselves up to God. God can do something for them.

The Roman Catholic Niece

Later on, while I was still pastor of the Evangelistic Tabernacle in El Cajon, California, God was good to us in those days. My! I was going to school most of the time that I was pastoring the church, working to make a living, and yet God gave us revival all the time it seemed like. Sunday school kept growing, and we always had a moving of the Spirit. But one Sunday morning that I preached, I noticed a certain family we had in the church. They were always good about bringing people to church. They brought more people to church and saw more people get saved than anybody I know. They took in foster children for the state, and they'd always bring them to church. The boys always got saved. I never saw anything like it.

Anyway, she had a Catholic niece visiting. She brought her to church. That morning, I preached. I generally did not give an altar call on Sunday morning. No reason! I generally just didn't do it. But this particular morning, I did give an altar call. And this lady's niece, a Catholic lady of about 35 years of age, had two twin boys, 14 years of age, with her. Besides others who came to the altar, this Catholic mother and her two boys came to the altar. It was their first time in any Protestant church, and it was an Assembly of God church. I had not said one word about the Holy Spirit baptism. But here was this Catholic lady, literally crying, crying out tears of repentance, asking God to save her. One of the most refreshing sights I've ever seen! And all of a sudden, on an impulse as the Lord spoke to me, I reached over and touched this Catholic lady. I said, "Sister, receive the Holy Spirit." Now I hadn't said one word about the Holy Spirit. No doctrine had been talked about. But as if she understood, this lady just easily raised both hands and with tears streaming down her face, she began to speak in tongues right there, kneeling at the altar.

I reached over and touched one of the boys. I said, "Son, receive the Holy Ghost." And just like his mother, he raised his hands, and he began speaking in tongues. God was moving in a wonderful way. People getting saved and filled with the Spirit! This is Holy Ghost revival! Hallelujah!

The lady's gone on to be with the Lord, now. We found out later that she lived for Christ for so many years and finally got her husband converted before she went to be with the Lord. God was moving in a wonderful way.

The Pattern for Revival

These things happen today when we believe. And truly, Samaria had received the Holy Spirit. This is the pattern for Holy Ghost revival. Preaching! Repentance! Confession of sins! Miracles! Healing! Conviction! Salvation! Filling of the Holy Spirit! When the word is believed, souls are saved. When the word is believed, the need for the Holy Spirit is seen. When the need for the Holy Spirit is seen, the Holy Spirit is received. And if you have not received the Holy Spirit, then you should. It's your privilege to receive the Holy Spirit.

Practical Factors

Now let me move on to some more practical factors in receiving the Holy Spirit. This is the pattern for Holy Spirit revival. The pattern for keeping revival is to practice the gift that God has given you. Practicing includes praying in tongues, seeking God, being earnest, and delighting yourself in the Lord. These keep revival going.

When it came to receiving the Holy Spirit in Samaria, as I previously mentioned, the apostles came down. I believe they talked to the people, told them what to expect, how God would move, and what their part was. I believe they discussed all of this. And that's what we've been trying to do meeting after meeting throughout our ministry, and pass on to you some of the things that God has shown us to help you understand how to yield yourself that you might be filled with the Holy Spirit—to take the "bugaboos"[7] out of it and the things that make you afraid so you can understand. We Pentecostal people, in some of our churches, have been so beat down. We have fears, neuroses and psychoses.

It's unimaginable, all that some Pentecostal people have in their hearts. They're scared to death! And we ought not be. For God has not given us the spirit of fear, but of power and of love and of a sound mind. Hallelujah! We ought to have the best minds in the business. All right?

False Expectations

Some people have a fear of doing something improper if they receive the Holy Spirit. Some people are afraid they might have to roll on the floor. And if you're from the old school—like some I've seen—I've seen plenty of that, all right, in my time. And it seemed that in some places they thought you ought to roll on the floor. Of course, I've always had a private interpretation on that. I've always thought some people like to see others roll on the floor, because at least they look better than those who are rolling anyway. They like to see others get messed up a little bit, you know, and thought they had to be humbled. No, you don't have to do that—don't have to do that at all. In fact, in my meetings, people generally never fall down. I just don't preach that way—that's all. I don't expect it.

And I've got nothing against people falling down! If you want to fall down, come, fall down. It's okay. It's your church. You're paying for it. It's your rugs. And I'm not being facetious, because I know it does happen. I've had people fall under my ministry. I've had people fall and be healed, as God moved! Yes, I have. I know what I'm talking about. All I'm saying is, "You don't have to fall!" Say me a good "Amen" to that.

You don't have to. That's what I call the domino theory. The first guy falls, then everybody else falls right in line. You don't have to do that. I was over in Juneau for a meeting. One fellow got the baptism in the Holy Spirit. He wanted to testify. He said, "I found out that I didn't go unconscious." No, you don't have to go unconscious. Some people think they will, but you don't. All right?

Many times, when we do strange things or improper acts, it's only our reaction to receiving the baptism. It's not that the Holy

Spirit makes us do it. Did you ever stick your finger in a light socket? Have you ever done that? Or have you ever seen anybody do it? It's a fun thing to watch. Particularly if you're not the guy. Oh, you can see a fellow do a jig until he gets it out of there. It's pretty dangerous. It's not recommended procedure—you understand!

Sailor's Reaction

I was on the cruiser USS *Galveston* in the Mediterranean back in 1967 when the Holy War[8] broke out. We went to sea for six weeks. Well, by that time, you do everything in the world to entertain yourself, you know. And so one night they broke out with music. We had a band which got together, and they began to sing on the forecastle deck. And they had their stuff all rigged up there. I mean they were wired for sound. Boy, they were really wired. And one fellow was going to sing. They put the microphone up, and he touched his lips with the microphone, and it shorted out. I'm telling you, he did a jig. He threw that thing as far as he could throw it. Now the fact is that he wasn't killed or hurt. But it was funny. Had he been killed, it would have been another story you know.

But now electricity didn't do that to him. That was his reaction to the electricity. That's all that was. And so when some people come into contact with the Holy Spirit, it's their own reaction you see. It's not that the Holy Spirit makes them react.

The Lutheran Girl

I was in Claremont in San Diego, preaching. In fact, every time I'm in town, I have an open invitation at the church there. No matter what's going on, I stop and preach. Over a hundred people have gotten the baptism there because I stop in every once in a while. They might have gotten saved since the last time, but we get them filled and keep them filled all the time. And that's the way it works there. They have a day school there through the eighth grade. And they had a young Lutheran girl who went to their school. She told her mother, "They have a revival going on over there! I want to go to the meeting." Her mother said, "You're not going down to that meeting and get that Holy Ghost. They'll have you falling on the floor in no time or what!" Well they were scared to death. Undoubtedly, they were Lutheran and saw something, somewhere, you know, that terrified them.

But the girl persisted and got to the meeting. And she came down, we laid hands on her, and she received a wonderful baptism. No falling down! Nothing! Then she said, "I want to go home and tell momma."

"Oh," the church said, "Don't you tell momma tonight. You wait 'til later."

But she went home and told momma anyway. She said, "Momma, I went to the meeting. And you know what? I received the Holy Ghost, and I didn't fall down either." She got that out real fast.

Her mother said, "Now, isn't that lovely?" She didn't have to fall down at all.

Holiness

Now some people think that holiness is a criterion for receiving the Holy Spirit. I've heard people say, "God won't fill an unclean vessel." Now doesn't that sound holy and good? Except, it just isn't true, that's all. The only thing is that there is something wrong with that statement.

I was invited to preach in the Pentecostal Holiness Church in Oakland, California. I got over there, and I said, "You really want me to preach on the baptism with the Holy Spirit?"

"Yeah!"

"Okay!"

And so, of course, their view of sanctification is horrendous. I entered into a real one on that one. And so while I was preaching,

I was telling them about holiness, that it is not a criterion for receiving the baptism with the Holy Spirit.

And the deacon said, "Chaplain, you're wrong! He said, "The Bible says God won't fill an unclean vessel." And he looked up victoriously.

I said, "Brother, is that right?"

He said, "That's right."

I said, "Okay, would you please find it in the Bible? I don't think it's there."

"Yeah, I'll find it." He took his Bible, and for 20 minutes he thumbed through the Bible. Finally, he said, "I can't find it. But I know it's there."

Well, it isn't there. That's all. It just plain isn't there! But, somehow, we picked it up and it sounded good. So everybody quotes it.

What is Holiness?

Now I've got to ask, what is holiness? Whose standard are we going by? Yours? I might not like yours. Or, mine? You probably wouldn't like mine. Or are we going by the standard of Assemblies of God? Nobody can live up to that one. What is it? What is the standard? Whose standard is right? I like mine better than I do yours. You might not even have any. Can't tell! But you've got a divine holiness.

So one day I got excited. I thought, "Well, I'm going to look this thing up. What is holiness?" You know, sometimes these thoughts get in your head, and you begin to say, "Well, now, let's just see what it is." And you know what I found out? I found that some think that if you want to be holy, you don't drink or smoke or chew. But the Bible says that God is holy. Does that mean He doesn't smoke, drink or chew? It can't mean that. He isn't holy just because he doesn't drink, smoke or chew. It doesn't mean that! Can't mean that! Holiness simply means one thing. It's a group or an individual or a unit set apart to itself for a particular purpose. That's what holiness means.

Now what does it mean when it says that God is holy? It simply means that God is holy in that He is set apart to Himself as opposed to anything else. He's holy in the sense that He's alone. What does it mean when it says Israel was holy unto the Lord? They were a bunch of bums! But they were holy in that God had chosen them to be a peculiar or a particular people. We are holy in that God has saved us and called us out to be the church. It doesn't mean we're perfect, or we do everything right. It means we've been a people separated unto God and for God's purposes. That's what holiness is.

Now don't misunderstand me. If you get straight with God and start living right, God will clean your life up. That'll follow suit. We're not decrying that. But we need to understand, basically, what holiness is. Amen? Now if we understand that, it removes a lot of our problems.

The US Marine Who Got Saved and Baptized in the Spirit

I was in Burbank, California—beautiful downtown Burbank. So I preached at a Christ Ambassador rally[9] there. And a Marine from Camp Pendleton Marine Base was there. He was the son of an Assembly of God minister. I didn't know this at the time. And so he came down. I thought he came down to get the baptism. So I started to lay hands on him.

He was a Baptist and he said, "I'm not even saved."

I said, "Well, get saved!"

He had blurted at me, so I just blurted back at him. Fair enough! And that Marine dropped to his knees and began praying. So I went on to pray with somebody else. After a few minutes, he reached down in his shirt pocket and took out a package of cigarettes and threw them across the altar. Then he raised his hands and began talking in tongues. Like I tell you about Marines, when you command them to get saved, they do! Hallelujah!

But let me tell you, he was going with a teenager in the church. That was the reason he was in church. A lovely young teenager invited him to church. He was going with her. And she wore mini-dresses and miniskirts. And so I found out a week later that he said to her that afternoon, "You're going to have to quit wearing miniskirts and start wearing longer skirts."

She said, "Wait a minute. We're not even engaged yet."

He said, "No, and we're not going to be 'til you learn how to dress."

That's the way God had affected this US Marine. Praise the Lord!

So perfect holiness cannot be a criterion, or none of us could receive the Holy Spirit. How about when you got saved? You didn't get all cleaned up and come to God to get saved, did you? No you didn't. You came just as you were, and God took you just as you were, and God cleaned you up.

And another thing, the Holy Spirit baptism isn't going to make you any better than you were. The blood of Jesus Christ, God's son, cleanses from all sin. And you're never going to be any more saved than you are. If you're saved, you're saved! Period! So we need to understand that.

But from there on, we "grow in grace, and in the knowledge of our Lord and Savior, Jesus Christ" (II Peter 3:18). It's a growth in grace as long as you live. Hallelujah!

I've heard some people say that when they got the baptism, particularly if they had to tarry a long time and be at the benches a while, when they finally got it, they said, "Thank God, I'm through." And they were!

The Lady Delivered from Tobacco

I've seen people who smoked get the baptism of the Holy Spirit. I was in Oxnard, California, at the church pastured by Rev. Elmer T. Draper. We had a good meeting there. Eight received the Holy Spirit. We we're getting ready to close the meeting out, and going to turn the lights out. And two middle-aged ladies came down the middle aisle. Both were heavyset ladies. One lady had her head in her hands, sobbing. I said, "What's the trouble?" I tell you, I thought, boy, it was something bad.

The lady who was sobbing couldn't even talk to me.

The other lady said, "Chaplain, she wants you to pray for her that God will deliver her from tobacco."

My first impression was, "Isn't it wonderful that somebody can be so concerned about something like that?" And so I said, "Sister, listen to me." She was so embarrassed. Can you imagine being embarrassed for smoking? So ashamed and embarrassed, she wouldn't even look at me! Finally, I put my hand under her chin and lifted her chin up. I said, "Open your eyes and look at me."

And she finally did, sobbing.

I said, "Sister, God loves you. God *loves* you. He doesn't want you to smoke, but He hasn't thrown you out of the family. You're still one of His. He loves you."

And about the third time I said that, I saw her lips begin to tremble. I put my hands on her head. I said, "Go ahead and talk in tongues."

She must have been from Oklahoma, 'cause boy, when I said that, she jumped about a foot in the air and ran up and down the aisle, shouting in tongues and having the time of her life. Hallelujah! She loved God, and God loved her. And when she realized that God did love her, she received the Holy Ghost that easily. And I would suppose that she's given up smoking.

Three years later, I spoke in Santa Clara, California, at the Neighborhood Church, pastored by Rev. T. Ray Rachels. I made this statement. I said, "Tonight, when I give the invitation to come forward, there'll be no criterion for holiness. There is no standard. If you tell me you're saved and love Jesus Christ, that's all I want to hear. That's enough." This shakes some people to death you know. Well, that night about three got the baptism and about three got healed. But that night, after the service, a lady told me who she was and said to me, "Chaplain, you were here three years ago and you did the same thing. At that time, you said holiness is no criterion. And I came down, you laid hands on me, and I received the Holy Spirit. At the time you laid hands on, I had the habit of tobacco, I drank, I swore." She laid it out.

I said, "How are you getting along now?"

"Well, I'm all cleaned up now," she said. Well, of course.

Instructions to Receiving

Now the days of tarrying are over. When hands are laid on you, your lips will begin to tremble. We call this *stammering lips* according to Isaiah 28:11. If at that moment you would not hinder it, that is if you would go with it, don't talk in English—physiologically and psychologically, you cannot speak two languages at one time; it's impossible. So if you make yourself speak English or your acquired language, you cannot speak in tongues—if you refuse to speak in your own language and talk out anything else, you'll be speaking in tongues in a matter of moments. Sure! That's the way it is. That's the message we're trying to get across.

You have to get your lips, your tongue, your vocal cords, and your breath in action. Get it in motion! Then God will fill you with the Holy Spirit.

May God bless these few thoughts to our hearts. And if there are those of you who would like to receive the Holy Spirit, we'd certainly be pleased to lay hands on you that you might receive.

Benediction

Father, we thank you for your goodness and your kindness to us. Bless we pray in Jesus' name. Amen.

6

WHY SPEAK WITH TONGUES?
1 CORINTHIANS 14

Review

Now let's review questions that we have discussed. I fielded questions from live audiences, and I'll give answers to them. In these series of messages, we have discussed the questions, "Does the Holy Spirit speak through a person when one speaks in tongues?" And we've decided that He does not. The Holy Spirit does not do the speaking. The individual does the speaking. For the Apostle Paul said, "if I pray in an unknown tongue, my spirit prayeth" (I Cor. 14:14). And so it's a person's own spirit that does the praying and his own vocal mechanism that does the speaking. And, of course, this solves once and for all the question, "Does the devil speak in tongues?" And, of course not. The devil does not speak in tongues, and neither does the Holy Spirit. The individual does the speaking in tongues. And this is scriptural. That removes a lot of fear from a person's heart. Some people are so afraid that God's going to come in, vertically, downward, and through their minds and through their mouths and talk. We're not made that way. We're made to cooperate with God and speak from the depths of our souls. I have been bringing to your attention that when you receive anything in these meetings, you are not receiving an absentee Spirit and calling Him down into you. Not at all.

The Holy Spirit is already within you. So we're calling him up to manifest the tongues as you yield yourself to the Holy Spirit. It's more simple this way, and more enjoyable, and not so scary when you understand it like this. Can you say a good "Amen?" Say it really good.

Now we also discussed the question, "Can a person get a wrong experience in seeking for the Holy Spirit?" And we came to the conclusion that one cannot get a wrong experience. And if you'll remember, I asked you the question, "What kind of a God are you serving anyway, if you've got to keep one eye on God and be sure He gives you the right thing?" Of course, the problem is, you wouldn't know what was right anyway. But Luke 11:13 says, "If ye then, being evil, know how to give good gifts unto your children, how much more shall your heavenly Father give the Holy Spirit to them that ask Him?" If you come to God seeking the Holy Spirit, that's exactly what you're going to get. He would not be God to let something else happen to you. The safest place in the world is seeking the face of God. Amen. How we ever let our minds get twisted to think otherwise, I don't know. But it has happened in Pentecostal circles. These kinds of thoughts are going around. And it scares good people—and rightly so. But the safest place is seeking God. Hallelujah! And you'll get what you've come to seek for.

In the last chapter we discussed the question, "Is holiness a criterion for receiving the baptism of the Holy Spirit?" And we came to the conclusion that holiness was not a criterion, if by that is meant the old business of "Don't drink, smoke or chew, wear short dresses, or have bobbed hair"[10]—that's what holiness means to some people. That's some people's idea of holiness. Well, if that's your idea of holiness, then holiness is not a criterion for receiving the Holy Spirit. For we've seen all kinds of people receive the Holy Spirit just because they love God and wanted God. And God filled them. And I'll tell you one thing—after you get filled with the Holy Ghost, you always have to grow in grace and knowledge of the Lord and Savior Jesus Christ as long as you live the rest of your life anyway. It's a matter of growth as long as you live. So holiness, as we understand it, is not a criterion for receiving the Holy Spirit. You come as you are, and God receives you as you are. Now aren't you glad to know that? Hallelujah!

Now if you understand holiness as being called and set apart to the glory of God, that's another thing. Anybody who's saved is holy in that sense of the word, in that he's called and he's part of the church. The church is a chosen vessel, a peculiar people. In that sense we're all holy. Now aren't you glad to find that you're holy? It's a good thing to find out.

And somebody said, "You mean me? You don't know me." Yeah, I know you. Sure do! I know you because I know me. And we're all made out of the same thing. All minds are just about alike. There's not too much difference. And if you know human nature at all, you know about everybody. That's about the way it is. So don't think that they're saying, "Well, oh, they don't know about me." Yeah, we all know about each other. Of course we do. But thank God we've been called. We're part of the church in that sense. We're holy because we're God's people. We're holy with all of our imperfections, with all of our wrongs, with all of our sins, with all of our shortcomings. He still calls us a holy people. Isn't that wonderful? It looks like you'd be glad to know that. But this is the way it is. Hallelujah! All right!

We've been emphasizing the fact that the baptism of the Holy Spirit is a doctrine of the New Testament by name and terminology. In Matthew 3:11, John stated, "I indeed baptize you with water unto repentance, but He that cometh after me is mightier than I, whose shoes I am not worthy to bear; He shall baptize you with the Holy Spirit and with fire." Now that's a good, strong term.

In Acts 1:5, Jesus said, "John truly baptized with water; but ye shall be baptized with the Holy Spirit not many days hence." Here Jesus, again, spoke of the baptism in the Holy Spirit. Then, in Acts 2, we saw the outpouring of the Holy Spirit, which there is called the baptism in the Holy Spirit. Tongues is part of it.

We saw it again in Acts 10 at the household of Cornelius. Cornelius and his family and friends received the baptism. And when Peter gave an explanation of it in Acts 11:16, he said, "Then remembered I the word of the Lord, how that he said, 'John indeed baptized with water but ye shall be baptized with the Holy Spirit.'" He called the event in Acts 10 by name, the baptism in the Holy Spirit. Three times this term is used and refers to the Holy Spirit baptism, and the phenomenon of tongues is always attending.

We saw it again in Acts 19, when Paul met the disciples of John the Baptist. And when he told them who Jesus was, he baptized them in water and they became Christians. Then he laid hands on them, and they received the Holy Spirit with the attendant manifestation of speaking in tongues. So I bring to your attention, again, that the New Testament pattern is that people should get saved and filled with the Holy Ghost with the evidence of speaking in tongues all at one time. I don't know how we in Pentecost divided this thing up.

Well, maybe I'm unkind. That's a possibility. If you remember, it was at the turn of the century that we even recovered the doctrine of the Holy Spirit baptism. And now we're interpreting that as a subsequent work rather than part of redemption. We're wrong there. However, it's part of the whole redemption story. And we see that it should take place at the time a person gets saved. And if no one's tampered with his religion, and no one's told him wrongly, he could receive it at the same time. Hallelujah! We've seen it everywhere we've been and preached this message.

Introduction

Now there are some things I want to bring to your attention. I was preaching in a church in Southern California some years ago, and the pastor of the church had a book. I don't know if he realized how good it was. But it was a book very old and out of print. It was so old, it wasn't even copyrighted. And these things were written in the 1800s. So we're not really new after all. Somebody has seen this truth ahead of us. I was with him in that church. And I sat down every day with a typewriter typing up the main thoughts in that book that I thought I needed to know. And some of these statements I thought I'd give to you in passing along here for you to remember.

This man said things concerning tarrying.[10] In relation to the Holy Spirit, this author said that *tarry* is not a New Testament word. Yet, thousands of poor Christians have spent years of unnecessary waiting for this baptism through thinking that it is a New Testament word. Some people still think you're supposed to tarry to receive the Holy Spirit. They're wrong. Now, before we go any further, let us try to remove a widespread misconception about these ten days of waiting. The 120 believers waited ten days before Pentecost. The command to tarry given to these first disciples, before the New Testament era began on the Day of Pentecost, is not a command to us today. Many act as if it were. And the loss to the Church through this mistake is incalculably and pitiably sad.

In one of our meetings we met people who had tarried 10, 20, or 30 years. In one meeting, we met one guy who tarried 42 years. He was a charter member of a church we were preaching in one time. He didn't know any better, and the church didn't know any better to tell him anything. They let him sit there and be like that for 42 years. Can you imagine?

The Pentecostal baptism is a present blessing. How many Christians believe this? Again and again, when we have set this before our people, and urged it earnestly, someone present has voiced the views of many with the following question—if it were necessary for those early disciples to tarry ten days before they could receive this fullness. I've heard this in old-time Pentecostal churches sometimes. On what ground do you argue that for them the tarrying is unnecessary? St. John gives to this question a beautiful answer. When Christ gave this command to the eleven, the Holy Spirit was not yet given, for that Jesus had not yet been glorified. The Holy Spirit had not yet come to his Church in New Testament fullness, and for this reason, they had to tarry. Hallelujah!

Then he asked the question, "But was not the Holy Spirit always in the world among men?" Certainly, but not in the measure in which He is with us now—in His own dispensation.

We are now living in the dispensation of the Spirit and may now, therefore, have the fullness of power for which the first Christians had to wait. God is not honored, and there is no blessing when men are waiting for months or years, as too many are doing, for that which God wants us to have, and which a perishing world needs to have today. Hallelujah!

In theory, the evangelical churches all believe this firmly. They are ever-ready to quote and endorse the text, "Not by might, nor by power, but by my Spirit, saith the Lord of hosts" (Zech. 4:6). The pity is that there is often such a wide gap between our creed and our conduct.

In reading the Acts of the Apostles, we can see clearly that even when the apostles led people to Christ through conversion, the apostles were not content. They never rested until they led them into the fullness of the Spirit. That's the way the New Testament Church operated.

While in most cases true love for Christ begins at the cross, our true service for Christ begins at Pentecost. The great reason so much earnest Christian work, prayer and sacrifice today yields such meager results is that a large portion of today's disciples of Christ are living on the wrong side of Pentecost. Chronologically, of course, they're on the right side, but experientially, they have not reached it yet.

We are often asked, "Have not all Christians the Spirit?" Certainly! "If any man have not the Spirit of Christ, he is none of His" (Rom. 8:9). But all are not filled with the Spirit. Having the Spirit and being filled with the Spirit are different things in degree. I think that's needful to understand. That's what we've been trying to get across.

In receiving the baptism there must be purity of motive. There must be a full and glad surrender. There must be implicit present trust. We sometimes wait even if we don't have to. Waiting is a pre-Pentecost command and does not refer to us at all. Trusting, not waiting, is a post-Pentecost prerequisite and is the medium through which this blessing comes.

Concerning feelings and receiving the baptism, we must not wait for feeling before we take God at His word. In seeking pardon, people often want to feel first and trust afterwards. And we often have some difficulty with many who seek this fuller blessing. They come to God with a set of preconceived notions for which they have no need. They expect that when He takes full possession, they will receive joyous thrills and marvelous spiritual shocks that will move their souls with "Hallelujah" earthquakes. We know that's not so, though, don't we!

Take Him at His word. Assume that He keeps His word and does His part, seeing you have done yours. Hold onto the bare Word of God, and all the feelings you need will come in the right way, at the right time. When I claimed my birthright, I had no ecstatic thrills and no extra joyous emotions. I knew my surrender was complete, and having taken God at His word, I was sure the experience was mine. I had tongues, though I felt little different otherwise. I was at peace, and the battle was over. Great feelings have come since. When the Church is filled with the Spirit, He will take care of the human cry for amusement and thrill. You won't have to pass laws against the various illegal amusements of the world, for you will not desire them. Can you say "Amen" to that?

As previously shared, in one of my last nights in the church in Juneau, a kind of a stately lady came forward and wanted the baptism. She had her Bible in her hand. I said, "Would you lay the Bible on the table?" She reluctantly did so. I said, "Now, will you open your mouth and speak in tongues?"

And she began to cry a little bit and said, "I don't want to do it. I want Him to do it."

I said, "Honey, He ain't gonna do it. You will have to do it." And she began to talk in tongues so easily.

But, you see, we have some people with preconceived notions that come and stand here just like concrete pillars, and God, all of a sudden, is supposed to make them start operating. We're not automatons. We're not robots. We're not machines. We're people with minds, people with hearts. He's asking for our cooperation, and that's more miraculous than making a statue speak. Don't you understand? The fact that we can cooperate with God and be used of God is a wonderful thing. This is the message we've been taking, literally, all around the world.

Now the subject is "Why Speak with Tongues?" I'm doing a lot of quoting tonight from various people, backing up the scriptural references of why we should speak in tongues.

Why Speak with Tongues—First Positive Statement

Now the first positive statement regarding speaking in other tongues comes when Paul, in I Corinthians 12:28, says, "God hath appointed in the church . . . various kinds of tongues" (NASB). Larry Christiansen, who was the pastor of the Lutheran church in San Pedro, California, and who is a Charismatic, wrote concerning this matter. His whole church is in this business of tongues. He said that even if this were the only passage that mentions speaking in tongues, we would have to conclude that it is of abiding value today, because God has ordained it so. Certainly, God does not ordain anything for His Church that is worthless, harmful, stupid, mad, or unimportant. There is the expression in I Corinthians 12:8-10 as well, "To one is given by the Spirit the word of wisdom . . . to another divers kinds of languages . . . ."

The Holy Spirit is the author of speaking in tongues, as it says expressly in I Corinthians 12:11, "all these worketh that one and the selfsame Spirit." According to its origin, then, tongues is a charisma, a gift from God.

Now one point I would add to this is that some people would say, "Yes, but if that's the only reference, you've got to be careful, because you really should have several references to prove a point."

That's not true at all. All Bible-believing Christians must believe in the gift. If it were only said once, they would believe it.

Let me illustrate. I bring to your attention to the fact of the virgin birth of Jesus Christ. That is mentioned only once in the New Testament, and that's in the Gospel of Matthew. And the Apostle Paul never talked about it once. But that doesn't make any difference. The fact that it is there means we accept it. Amen? Sure. So when some scholars tell you that the gift of tongues is mentioned only once (though it's mentioned more than once) and that, therefore, it is not relevant today, that's no argument. For the person who believes in Scripture, if it's said only once, that's all you need anyway, because it's the Word of God.

And don't ever fall into this trap. Somebody will say, "Yeah, but you have to be careful. Some of the writers in the Bible and some of their writings may be a little more inspired than the others." This is not true. All of the Scriptures are equally inspired. And what Paul said is as important as what Jesus said.

Now there's a school of thought that says, "What Jesus says is more important than the rest." That's not true. The whole Bible is inspired, for the same Holy Spirit who moved through Jesus Christ when He was here is the same Holy Spirit who moved through the apostles when they were here. Hallelujah! We need to understand this.

Why Speak with Tongues—Second Positive Statement

The second positive statement is in I Corinthians 14:2, which states, "For he that speaketh in an unknown tongue speaketh not unto men, but unto God." Paul is saying that one utters mysteries in the Spirit, for "if I pray in an unknown tongue, my spirit prayeth" (I Cor. 14:14). Paul maintains that the spirit dwelling in man speaks to God in a way that is incomprehensible to man. That is, it bypasses his own intellect. But because the Spirit dwells in us and infuses our whole being, our total person is caught up in this praying, which is more direct and total than prayer with the mind.

Paul expresses this in Romans 8:26 and 27, "for we do not know how to pray as we should; but the Spirit Himself intercedes for us with groanings too deep for words; and He who searches the hearts knows what the mind of the Spirit is, because He intercedes for the saints according to the will of God" (NASB).

Besides this prayer with the spirit, prayer with the mind also has its rightful place. Paul says in I Corinthians 14:15, "I will pray with the Spirit, and I will pray with the understanding also. I will sing with the Spirit, and I will sing with the understanding also." Now this is all found in I Corinthians Chapter 14.

Why Speak with Tongues—Third Positive Statement

Now let's move on. A third positive statement is found in I Corinthians 14:4 where Paul the Apostle states, "He that speaks in an unknown tongue edifies himself." Now I'm going to give you a pretty important statement here. I want you to pay attention. The word *edification* may sound rather pious to us, but it is not. This is not true of the original Greek word. Arnold Bitlinger of Germany, incidentally, who has done a scholarly work in this area, says that what is meant here is the constructive building up of the personality. Now let me say a word. I tend to get facetious here. In our churches, a lot of our people surely do need some constructive building up of the personality, don't they! Some of our people are blah personalities. Right? That's right. Some of you would do well to get so filled with the Spirit that it would change your personality, make you outgoing and loving people, people who want to help other people, want to be good to people, and want to do something for God. That's what this is all for. Hallelujah!

Dr. Walter J. Hollenweger, the executive secretary of the Department on Studies in Evangelism in the World Council of Churches, characterizes these effects of speaking in tongues as the psycho-hygienic function of speaking in tongues. Now that's a mouthful. What he's saying here is that speaking in tongues brings healing and is therapeutic. Well, again, some of us need to get our minds healed, don't we? Get rid of some of the neuroses and psychoses and depressions that we let ourselves fall into. There's a reason for tongues, my friend—the psycho-hygienic function of speaking in tongues. He writes, "Man needs a non-intellectual means of meditation and release." You can do this when you're driving the car. You women can do it when you're doing the dishes or doing the clothes. No matter what you're doing, you don't have to think about it when you're speaking in tongues, because it's direct—from your spirit to Almighty God Himself. Hallelujah! That's why it's so valuable. It's a non-intellectual means of meditation and release.

Friedrick Heiler, the German theologian, thinks that pouring out one's heart to God has the effect of an inner release that goes beyond the contribution of psychoanalysis. Well, that's a pretty good statement. However, I would bring to your attention that of all the work that has been done in psychoanalysis, from Freud down to the present time, there is not one reported cure due to psychoanalysis. Not one! And yet people are sure putting the money into it. I'll tell you, if you want to get a cure, come to Jesus Christ and sell out to Christ and be filled with the Holy Ghost. Hallelujah! All right!

Now Arnold Bitlinger says there's a group of psychoanalysts, especially from the school of C.G. Jung, who confirmed the therapeutic effect of speaking in tongues.

Morton Kelsey, a theologian and psychotherapist, writes, "There are people who, without this experience, would never have been able to come to psychological maturity. The experience of speaking in tongues opened them up to the unconscious and to a fuller life."

That's what these people are saying.

Dr. Lincoln Vivier wrote a doctoral dissertation on speaking in tongues a few years ago, for the Department of Psychiatry at the University of Johannesburg in South Africa. Through his research, he was to establish whether or not healthy or basic personalities engaged in the experience of *glossalalia*, or as we say, *speaking in tongues.* Not only did Vivier discover that the Christians he examined were completely healthy and normal people, but also that they were better equipped to endure tension. A linguist with psychological training writes, "Speaking with tongues is one evidence of the Spirit of God working in the unconscious and bringing one to a new wholeness, a new integration of the total psyche, a process which the Church has traditionally called sanctification."

Larry Christiansen, the Lutheran, again says, "When someone prays in tongues, he is built up in that area of his life." Oh, what these people are saying is wonderful, isn't it!

I read Dr. Paul Tournier's book, *The Meaning of Persons.* If you get a chance to read it, read it. In fact, anything Tournier has written is well worth reading. He's a Swiss psychiatrist and a Christian. Tournier makes this statement:

> In the New Testament, we read the wonderful dialogues through which Jesus transforms the lives of those whom He meets, drawing out the person buried beneath the personage and revealing personal contact to them. In the New Testament we witness the growth of real community in the early church. Glossolalia or speaking with tongues, which played such an important part then, and which is still found in modern communities, appears to answer to the need of the spirit to express the inexpressible, to carry the dialogue with God beyond the narrow limits of clearly intelligible language.

We may conclude from this that, because it is God who has appointed speaking in tongues, because it is the Holy Spirit who inspires tongues, because speaking in tongues increases the possibility of a deepened prayer life, and because speaking in tongues contributes towards the spiritual development of the personality, Paul the Apostle can state in I Corinthians 14:18, "I thank God that I speak in tongues more than you all." And I Corinthians 14:5 literally states, "I desire that you all speak in tongues." How does Paul dare desire this? Only if it really is a charisma, that is, a gift, that is granted, in principle, to all Christians. Christiansen assumes this when he writes: "I am convinced that every Christian who desires this blessing can ask God for it and receive it." Hallelujah!

Now, that's from men who've made a study of this thing from various parts of the world. And these are conclusions they've come up with, of course, taking into consideration the fact that it exists anyway in the New Testament. We depend upon the New Testament for our source. But it's interesting to see what studies have been made and see how the Scriptures have been borne out.

Now let's look at the scriptural context of I Corinthians 14:2, which states, "he that speaks in an unknown tongue speaks not unto men, but unto God; for no man understands him. Howbeit, in the Spirit he speaks mysteries." What the apostle is saying here is that by the natural intellect, we don't know what we're saying when we speak in tongues, because we don't know the language. But from the very soul of man, I like to call it from the subconscious, we're praying from "the real you," directly to God Himself—your spirit making contact with the Spirit of God. And we speak mysteries or secrets that are not known even to our normal mental processes. I tell you one thing about it, our mentality has certainly crossed us up and goofed us up in more areas than one, hasn't it? Speaking in tongues is one thing the natural mentality can't goof up, because it can't get into it. It's from deeper down than that.

Now in I Corinthians 14:4, about edification, I've heard people say, "Well, it's better to edify the church than to edify yourself!" Doesn't that sound noble? It just isn't true. How can you edify the Church until you first get edified? And so in verse 4 Paul the Apostle states, "He that speaks in an unknown tongue edifies himself, but he that prophesies edifies the Church." The speaking in tongues is to edify yourself! To help yourself! To build up your own personality! Get you in contact with God, directly! And that's necessary before we can edify the Church or anyone else.

Gibberish

Now one thing I'd like to give to you is quite a revelation to some people. When it comes to speaking in tongues, some people are afraid they can't do it, or that what comes out may not really be a language. You know, friends, we have little faith. We really don't have much faith at all. We have to have faith in the operation of God.

The fact of the matter is, if any of you have done any traveling, you know as well as I do, any language that you don't understand sounds foolish. If I'd hear a Russian talk, it would sound silly, because I don't understand Russian. It would just be gibberish as far as I'm concerned. But if I heard English, or Spanish, some German, Greek text, some of these I would recognize because I've studied. And it wouldn't sound foolish. But if you don't know the language, it sounds foolish. And because we don't know the language, we think, "Well, we're just making it up, and it seems too easy the way the chaplain has been presenting this."

But in I Corinthians 14:10 is the key to this whole thing. Paul the Apostle states, "There are, it may be, so many kinds of voices in the world, and none of them is without signification." That means there is not anything you utter that would not have a meaning to God. Anything! Any kind of thing you would breathe out! Any kind of thing you would say! No matter how foolish it sounds, it would have meaning as far as God is concerned. Now you need to understand that.

So when you start talking in tongues, and it sounds kind of foolish and silly or like gibberish, and you don't think it's a language, remember this: There is not anything you can utter that doesn't have meaning as far as God is concerned.

I was in Newport, Rhode Island, three or four years ago now, attending a senior course. And in this particular course, a good friend of mine from Indiana University Northwest was there to speak to us chaplains on voice—how to speak. And he also had to sit in and judge a class when we did some speaking. And in my particular part of the speaking, I spoke on the Holy Spirit, and it was well received by him. He wanted to talk with me, privately, about it. And he was already favorable to the Holy Spirit message anyway, which was wonderful.

He said, "I'll give you another one to add to your repertoire. When a baby lies in the crib, a baby has a way of making his wants known, even though he does not have a structural language. And any mother can tell you what the baby wants, without even looking at him, just hearing him in the other room! She knows what he wants. He either wants something to eat or he's got a wet diaper or something else is the matter. But she knows what's going on!" Sure, they do. And the child has no structural language. He said, "Stan, that's the way it is when you speak in tongues. You don't wait until you get a structural language. You just start with what you have, and then the structured language comes." I thought that was beautiful. Hallelujah! And so you don't wait for this, you just start talking out.

There's one more thing I want to say about gibberish. I'm not running down the Baptists now. I'm running down Pentecostals now. I can talk about us because I'm one of us. Now I've heard Pentecostals say that when we get people talking in tongues, that's just gibberish, that it's not a real language. Now my first question is, "How do you know so much? Just how do you?"

Larry Christiansen was over in Germany, and he spoke with Dr. Theodore Rapp, professor of languages at Mainz University in Germany. Dr. Rapp spoke 8 languages fluently and worked in many others. And he's done some work in the tribal languages down in Africa. But Larry asked Dr. Rapp, "Doctor, if someone who was going to speak in tongues spoke gibberish, would you know? Could you tell if it was?"

Now this great linguist made this point. He said, "No, I couldn't, not unless I had 16 typewritten pages of phonetic script and heard it spoken for a great number of times. Not even then could I decide." But how does a common individual on the street of America decide that it's gibberish when he doesn't know anything or hasn't got half the mind that Dr. Rapp has got? We're just talking through our hats. We don't know what we're talking about. We're silly. Don't be too quick to call anything gibberish. You don't know, not unless you're a linguist. And you know, before you say anything is not a language, you've got to speak about 6,000 languages, because there's about that many languages and dialects in the world today. So until you speak them all, don't call anything gibberish. You plain don't know. I don't hear anyone saying "Amen." Yes, this is the way it is.

So all utterance has meaning to it. The difficulty is that we need to have faith in God's Word and trust it to be true. Then we'll see things begin to work. How wonderful it is to see somebody who has never spoken in tongues. They don't know how. You lay hands on them, you tell them to utter anything, they begin to utter something. Then all of a sudden they go in a language and assume a language, and move right along. This is the way it works. You don't wait 'til you have a perfect language. You start with what you've got, and God takes over and helps you.

Interpretation

Let's discuss I Corinthians 14:13, regarding tongues and interpretation. I'm throwing this issue in the discussion because it comes up from time to time. Several people have expressed concern to me that when they went to various churches, and the Lord moved upon them to give a message in tongues, nobody interpreted it for them! And they were hurt that the church was so "unspiritual" as not to have somebody interpret their message.

Well now, I'll tell you what. If you ever fall into a category like that, and you go to a church and you speak in tongues, we have a little do-it-yourself kit right here. For it says in verse 13, "let him that speaks in an unknown tongue pray that he may interpret." So if no one interprets it for you, you get up and interpret it. "Me?" "Yeah, you!" You're the one that had the nerve to talk in tongues. Of course, we're pretty safe when we talk in tongues, because nobody knows what we're saying anyway. But if you give a message, or even the interpretation, you at least have got to be half right! Or somebody's going to nail your ears to the wall! No, they wouldn't either because we haven't got anybody spiritual enough or bold enough to jump on somebody if they made a mistake anyway. And that's what Paul the Apostle says you're supposed to do about a prophet. If a prophet gets up and says something wrong, somebody who knows the Bible is supposed to get up and set him straight. That's what Paul the Apostle taught. I don't know what has happened to our Church since then. It does not happen constructively today. Today, we'd split him wide open, wouldn't we? Fireworks! You bet we'd have fireworks, because none of us are very spiritual anyway. But we're far below the New Testament norm. This is what the Bible says: "let him pray that he may interpret."

Incidentally, the best writers on the subject are giving advice like this: if you visit some assembly where you are not known, and you don't know the assembly, it's better that you don't participate in the gifts of the Spirit in that church. That's right! Because, you don't know them and they don't know you. But in your own church you do know each other. And not only that, when a person goes to another church, the people of that church don't even know how the person's living. It's better that everything takes place in the local church where everybody knows everybody. Amen? That's the best reading and the best writing on it. So if you do speak in tongues, you be ready to interpret in case somebody doesn't do it for you.

So this is the way the Scripture reads, and this is the way the Scripture instructs us to carry out things. Also if a church is alive and spiritual, the gifts of the Spirit should be in evidence in the church. There should be tongues and interpretation and prophecy. This is all right. It should be that way. However, if there is the gift of tongues in the church, there ought to be not over three, and there ought to be an interpretation for each one. That's what the Bible says.

I know of a church in the San Diego area. In one service one night they had 53 messages in tongues. That's utterly ridiculous. Foolish! A waste of good time! They were not saying anything new anyway. Really! But the Bible says, ". . . let it be by two, or at the most by three, . . . and let one interpret. But if there be no interpreter, let him keep silence in the church; and let him speak to himself, and to God" (I Cor. 14: 27, 28). That's what the Book says. Amen?

And then it says to "Let the prophets speak two or three, and let the other judge" (I Cor. 14:29). What does it mean to judge? It means just what it says. It's possible for a good person to have the anointing of the Spirit of prophecy and say something wrong. And it doesn't mean he's a bum. It doesn't mean he backslid. It doesn't mean anything like that. It may be that he just went beyond his own knowledge and went wrong on the thing! Then, whoever's got the knowledge of the Word of God ought to get up and set the thing straight and say what the Scripture says. And if the prophet is spiritual, he ought to acknowledge what the Word of God says as being true. Surely, what would happen is the prophet would quit the church and go join something else. He'd be so embarrassed, which means he would not be very spiritual anyway. It wouldn't take much to make us all quit and run away. No, we're a pretty shallow bunch. Right? Yeah, we are. We ought not be, but we are.

Two Ways of Praying

Now in I Corinthians 14:15, Paul the Apostle states that there are two ways of praying: "What is it then? I will pray with the Spirit, and I will pray with the understanding also." Those of you who have received the baptism of the Holy Spirit, I encourage you in your daily private prayer life to pray both ways—with your mind and with the Spirit. I'm a firm believer that people ought to pray in tongues every day. Some of us don't think so. Some don't practice it. Finally, it goes by the wayside. Finally, we've lost the gift we've had. We don't exercise it. In nearly every meeting I'm in, somebody who hasn't spoken in tongues for 20 years gets the ability renewed. It ought to be part of your private daily prayer life. It ought to be part of you while driving the car, doing the dishes, or whatever you're doing. You can pray that way no matter what you're doing. And friends, in the Spirit you're doing something beyond your own intelligence, beyond what you know is being accomplished.

Control Your Spirit

This statement from Paul the Apostle, "The spirits of the prophets are subject to the prophets," holds true for all the gifts. You may exert control over yourself at all times. The Holy Spirit does not come down and take hold of you and make you do anything against your will. You have to want to do it, for you are in control of your own spirit.

Now if God were moving in you and controlling you like a ventriloquist, then there would be no reason for Paul to write I Corinthians 14, for this chapter is a corrective chapter against the abuses of the gifts of the Spirit. And if it was all God, there wouldn't be any abuses, because God would do everything perfectly. But since we have something to do with our self, and we can make mistakes, then we're given some correctives so we know how to do and what to do. And the more spiritually-minded we are, the more we'll be able to take correction and get things straight in our lives and in the church.

Sandia Base

Now I would like to tell you about my trip to the Pentagon to speak on the baptism with the Holy Spirit—one of the most outstanding things in my life I suppose. In 1968, I was in San Diego, and I was leaving the USS *Galveston*, a cruiser. But in March 1968, I was part of 20 Navy senior chaplains, and 80 more Army and Air Force senior chaplains—that's colonels and lieutenant colonels in the Air Force and the Army, and captains and commanders in the Navy. I was selected with the one hundred to go to Sandia Base[11] over in Albuquerque, New Mexico, to attend the Eighth Military Chaplains Nuclear Training Course, sponsored by the Defense Atomic Support Agency. Authorities were going to tell us just what capabilities we had. Brethren, I'll tell you, it's frightening what we do have—more than you think and know.

Anyway, one of the chiefs of chaplains usually comes out to greet the group. This particular year, the Chief of Navy Chaplains was supposed to meet with us and talk with all of us. He could not come, and so he sent his deputy over to be in the seminar with us.

This deputy, Commander Bob Warren, was a very personal friend of mine. We had come into the Navy together many, many years before. I did not know he was coming, because I didn't know the chief had had to bow out. But, of course, this deputy knew I was coming and we'd been just about like brothers ever since we'd met. We'd always had a grand time together and a good spirit of fellowship between us. He is a Presbyterian. However, we got over to Sandia Base, and he met me when the plane touched down. We had a grand bear hug and a handshake and talked faster than women when we got together, I'll tell you for sure.

We got up into his room. All of a sudden he sobered up, and he said, "Stan, I've been tapped."

I said, "Tapped? What do you mean?"

He said, "I received the Holy Ghost."

I said, "You did?"

"Yes!"

I said, "Well, Bob, did you speak in tongues?"

He said, "No, but I've got it."

Well, I didn't feel pressed to go into it with him at that moment. This man is one of the sharpest men I've seen, used to be a line officer, a communicator in the Navy, and is one of the most comical men I have ever met in my life. Anything the guy says is

funny. He's a comedian without trying to be. And the language he uses is Navy language all the way, and he's salty, and he's funny.

So we talked a bit further that night, and then I went to my room. And the next morning we met for breakfast. And then we were in a seminar all day, being told about the nuclear power. Then that night we went out for dinner. But the Lord began talking to my heart, that I should talk to this chaplain about the Holy Spirit. And so we went back up into his room later that evening. And we got to talking about the Holy Spirit again. And after he talked a little bit, I looked him right straight in the eye. I said, "Bob."

He said, "What?"

I said, "The Lord has impressed me that I should lay hands on you to receive the baptism with the Holy Spirit."

He said, "He did?"

I said, "Yes, He did."

I said, "Bob," and I told him just what I've been telling you— "when I lay hands on you, your lips will begin to tremble." (Now this is a Presbyterian commander in the Navy.) "In Isaiah 28:11 that's what we call stammering lips. Bob, if at that moment you wouldn't hinder it, or you'd just go with it, I'll be speaking in tongues; take a word from me if you want to, and you'd be speaking in tongues in a matter of moments."

He said, "Gee, I will?"

I said, "Yes, Bob, you will."

And we talked on a little bit further. Finally, he put his hands on hips, he looked at me right straight in the eyes, and he said, "All right, do it!"

I said, "All right, kneel down!"

What I like about the military is that you don't fool around. You really get down to business when you decide what to do. And so we both knelt down by one of the bunks in the room there. We were side by side.

He said, "Stan, just a minute. Before you pray, I've had a bad back for years. Pray that God will touch my back, too."

I said, "Yeah, we'll take that in too, Bob."

And so, just like a little kid, he put his hands on the bunk, folded, like he's going to say, "Now, I lay me down to sleep." And I put my hand on his back. I said, "God, fill him with the Holy Ghost."

And just as I finished that, the Spirit of God hit this Navy commander. He jumped straight up like that and at the top of his voice began to speak in tongues. Hallelujah! It's a wonder that whole bachelor officers' quarters didn't hear us down there! We were talking loudly enough for all of them. And I was speaking in tongues, too. We were having a time.

It got funny. All at one moment, we both quit exactly the same moment, and turned and faced each other, and broke out laughing. It was the funniest thing I ever saw, to see this little sawed-off shrimp talking in tongues. A Presbyterian! And we laughed, "Haw haw," just laughed. It was funny.

Then all of a sudden he sobered up and he said, "Hey, can I do it again?"

I said, "Yeah, Bob, you can do it again. Go ahead."

So he did. He went on, again. Well, after that I went back to my room.

The next morning, he came down for breakfast. Oh, he was all joy. He greeted me and said, "Hey, Stan! When you left last night, I went to bed talking in tongues, and I got up talking in tongues." He said, "I can talk in tongues any time I want to." I said, "That's right, Bob." He learned something that some of us haven't learned yet.

Of course you can talk in tongues any time you want to. It's your gift, you see. Well, we were studying nuclear power by day, but we had the real power by night. I'm going to tell you for sure. We were talking in tongues and getting a hold of God. That's where the real power was, in the Holy Ghost.

Well, the week was over. From Sandia Base, some of the other chaplains and I had to go back to the coast of California. And the Navy sent a plane after us that should have been junked 20 years before. It was no good. It was worn out. It had seen its days. Even when the pilot put it down, he couldn't kill the engines because he was afraid he couldn't get them started again. Thankfully, we made it back. We didn't reach our destination, but they put it down at Miramar Naval Air Station. And we made it home from there. So we went our ways. This must have been February of 1968.

Pentecost in the Pentagon

So then in March, I was in San Diego. I received a phone call. Bob and I used to talk with each other about once a week on the autovon.[12] He said, "Hey, Stan! Can you come to Washington?"

I said, "Come to Washington? For what?"

He said, "I've got it all ready set up that you're to preach in the Pentagon on the baptism in the Holy Spirit."

I said, "You mean, take my annual leave and my money and come back there?"

"Well, gee," he said, "Yeah."

I said, "I don't know if I can arrange it."

He said, "Will you pray about it?"

I said, "Yeah, I'll pray about it. Sure. I'll let you know."

Well, of course, when you see these things happen, you know how you get. And so we got to thinking, "Well, yeah, we guess we could." So I called up and said, "Okay, Bob! I'm coming to Washington." I told him what day I'd be there. I said, "Get it lined up now. We'll be ready to go."

"Oh, we're ready," he said.

So I said, "Okay."

I took leave in May. We drove down through Savannah, Georgia, picked up a daughter of mine, went on up to Washington where we stayed in his home. And the next morning, May 15, he said, "We have to go to the Bureau of Naval Personnel. I have it lined up. You're going to speak there, first, at the executive dining area. That's where the admirals eat. You'll speak there tomorrow morning." I said, "Okay."

I was in civilian clothes. And so we went over, and we had breakfast together, and he introduced me. I took my New Testament out of my top pocket and just began to preach on the baptism in the Holy Spirit. And it was quite a group sitting there. Now these people had to go to work at eight o'clock. But I finished a little early. So after I finished, not knowing exactly who was there, I said, "Now, if we have time, and anybody should desire, and we had the place, we could lay hands on for people to receive the baptism of the Holy Spirit."

A Marine fighter pilot by the name of Major Myrl Allinder sat there. He was a major and highly decorated. He said, "Why can't you do it now?"

I said, "We can, come on!"

This Marine got up, came down and knelt right on the floor. Bob Warren, Carl Wilgus, and I laid hands on this Marine fighter pilot. He raised his hands and began talking in tongues right there in the Bureau of Naval Personnel. I was in civilian clothes, and he did not realize I was a Navy chaplain.

Then a civil servant, middle-aged lady, said, "Would you please pray for me to receive the baptism?"

I said, "Certainly!"

We laid hands on her, and she received a wonderful baptism. This lady did not know, and none of us knew at that time, of the severe tragedy that she was to undergo due to the loss of a loved one. It was a severe tragedy. But God gave her the Holy Spirit in time to take her through that tragedy and helped her keep her senses and keep her mind. Oh, God's good isn't He?

Now, I'll tell you what the Marine later said. This Marine fighter pilot in July 1971 was the escort for General Ralph E. Haines, Jr., the Continental Army Commander, who was the keynote speaker for a Full Gospel Business Men's meeting in Buffalo, New York. And the Marine made this statement which was partially quoted in *Voice Magazine*. He stated,

On May 14, 1968, I had been up all night that Tuesday night reading John 14, and crying out to God that I had no power to witness. Finally, exhausted, I took a shower around 5 a.m. and got ready to go to the Navy Annex where Commander Carl Wilgus, USN, had started a Wednesday morning prayer breakfast in the Bureau of Naval Personnel (BUPERS) Admiral's dining room. That Wednesday, however, I was not interested in prayer, but only in getting something to eat and gutting out another day at Headquarters Marine Corps after a sleepless night. My eggs finished, I was ready to leave when a 'stranger' in civilian clothes stood up in the back of the dining room, Bible in hand, and announced: 'The Holy Spirit just spoke to me, and told me to read you a Scripture.'

I was terrified! I knew what his Scripture was going to be! John 14! 'I tell you the Truth: he that believes on me, the things I do, he will do, and greater things, because I am going to my Father' (NIV).

When the stranger finished reading John 14:12-15, I asked him, 'How is it possible to do what Christ did? I can't even tell another Marine that Jesus loves him!'

The stranger answered, 'You need to be baptized by Jesus in the Holy Spirit.'

I fell on my knees and cried out, 'What is to prevent me from being baptized right now?'

The stranger said, 'Nothing.'

Then he came over and laid hands on my head. His hands were like two burning branding irons! Fire went through and over my body... the imprint of his two hands burned on my head day and night for two weeks! As the fire burned over and through me, I became terrified again, seeing my sins and need for the Savior. I tried to say, "Depart from me. I'm a wicked man." But all I could hear was, "I love you!"

I was overwhelmed with the mercy and presence of God's love, and my hands started to come up in the air. As my hands reached the 'position of the cross,' the un-Marine-like position of total surrender, I felt suddenly free, and I tried to say, 'Thank you, Father.' But what came out was something else. I was speaking and praying in another language.

After a few words, the stranger hushed me and said, 'That's enough. Pray silently, because there is no one to interpret what you are saying.'

Later, I learned the "stranger" was Captain Stan Linzey, CHC, USN. Commander Bob Warren, CHC, USN, was standing beside me when I began speaking and praying in tongues, and he told me I was speaking in Hebrew.

Nine years later, in 1977, in South Carolina, my wife and I would lay hands on my estranged German-Jew mother from California, who would instantly be saved and begin speaking and praying in another language. She then returned to California to begin leading my three sisters and their families to salvation. Two years after that, the Holy Spirit 'drove' me from Quantico, VA, to Florida to find my alcoholic dad, whom

I thought was dead. By a great series of miracles, I found my dad, who was saved on 6 July 1979. And in November 1979, he himself was baptized in the Holy Spirit at 4 a.m. in our hotel room in Tampa!

He then went on to tell how God used him to testify for Christ following this experience and how he witnessed in Vietnam. He said, "Because I'm a Marine fighter pilot, I understand physical power. But what I couldn't understand was my lack of spiritual power." And that baptism is when he got the spiritual power. I received a letter from Major Allinder since then in which he said, "Stan, I am considering resigning my commission after 15 years of service and going into the ministry and preaching on the baptism in the Holy Spirit." That's what happened as a result of this occasion at the Bureau of Naval Personnel on the first day.

Afterward, Bob said, "Tomorrow morning we go to the Pentagon."

I said, "Fine, let's go."

And so we got up bright and early and they had an amphitheatre there where they have regular lectures. These guys filed in and sat. They were there and seated in just a moment. The Pentagon is an awesome thing. During the war, 50,000 people worked there daily. That's a pretty good sized city in itself. They have 17 miles of corridors in that thing. It's a huge place with shopping centers in the building.

So I was introduced, and I began preaching on the baptism in the Holy Spirit. Well this time we had questions and answers, and we ran up to the eight o'clock deadline. They scattered in a minute. So we didn't get a chance to pray. I thought, "Boy, we've missed this one, haven't we?" But God was working out something else.

I went back to the chaplain's home. He was on duty. He went down to his office, and in a couple of hours he said, "Stan, can you stay over until tomorrow?"

I said, "No, I can't."

He asked, "Why? I've got 12 people who want us to lay on hands."

I said, "Bob, it's impossible." I was to go down to Springfield to one of our chaplains' conferences. So I said, "I'll tell you what to do."

He said, "Okay."

That night we took his tape recorder, and I cut a tape. I told him what to do and how to lay on hands. He said, "I'll memorize it." I'm sure he did. I got word from him later that many had received the baptism as he laid on hands. He laid hands on a girl who had a hole in her heart. She was instantaneously healed. I received letters from him since. He went to the USS *Columbus*, a cruiser, and had revival on the *Columbus*. People received the baptism on that ship. His wife had never received. Finally, in May 1973, I received a letter. He said, "Jenny has received the Holy Spirit since I laid hands on her." God began moving in that fellow's life, all as a result of our going there and following the will of God.

Well it made me realize how important it is to know the leading of the Holy Spirit and follow it. Incidentally, have you seen the little book about the general speaking in tongues? The Assemblies of God puts it out. General Haines, a 4-Star General, who was the number two man in the United States Army, received the baptism in the Holy Spirit. The Marine major, the fighter pilot whom I laid hands on, was an escort beside the general when he received the Holy Spirit at the Full Gospel Business Men's rally in Buffalo, New York. You will never know how far this thing will go, will you? When God begins to move, things begin to happen. Friends, we're living in great days, believe me. These are good days to be alive in, and to let God have his way in our lives.

7

AFTER TONGUES, WHAT?
GALATIANS 5

In this chapter, we're going to deal with a subject not concerned with tongues at all, but rather with walking in the Spirit. And so I want to share with you from Galatians Chapter 5.

Galatians 5:16 - 26 states,

This I say then, walk in the Spirit, and ye shall not fulfill the lust of the flesh. For the flesh lusteth against the Spirit, and the Spirit against the flesh; and these are contrary the one to the other, so that ye cannot do the things that you would. But if ye be led by the Spirit, ye are not under the law. Now the works of the flesh are manifest, which are these: adultery, fornication, uncleanness, lasciviousness, idolatry, sorcery, hatred, strife, jealousy, wrath, actions, seditions, heresies, envyings, murder, drunkenness, revelings, and such like: of the which I tell you before, as I have also told you in time past, that they which do such things shall not inherit the Kingdom of God. But the fruit of the Spirit is love, joy, peace, long-suffering, gentleness, goodness, faith, meekness, self control: against such there is no law. And they that are Christ's have crucified the flesh with the affections and lusts. If we live in the Spirit, let us also walk in the Spirit. Let us not be desirous of vain glory, provoking one another, envying one another.

May God bless this portion of His word to our hearts and minds.

Conversion

My personal experience was that at the age of nine I was converted in a Southern Baptist church down in South Texas. In those years, in Texas, if you were not a Baptist, somebody had tampered with your religion, because everybody that was anybody was a Baptist in those days. A Sunday School teacher took me to the altar and asked me, "Don't you want to go to the altar?" And of course, I said, "Yes." So I did. But I shall never forget when I prayed; I said, "Lord, you have weighed my life and saved my soul." And then I added, "But don't make a preacher." Somehow I had the sense that He was going to do just that.

I was in the Baptist church all through my teen years and won souls to Jesus Christ. I have a very warm spot in my heart for the Baptists. Not only that, but all of my education has been in the Baptist colleges and the Baptist seminaries as well as the Harvard Divinity School.

The time came that I entered the Navy as an enlisted musician just out of high school. I served in the Navy for eight years as a musician. For a period of time I had backslid, and then I got back to God. When I met Verna Hall, the thing to do would be to go to church, and so I went with her. I tell you girls, if you have a boyfriend on the string, hang in there. He'll do anything you want him to do. That's right. So don't give up. Just hold steady, and you'll win.

The Call to Preach

At church with Verna, I went to the altar and renewed my fellowship with Christ, and He renewed the call on my life to preach. And I said, "Okay, that's what you want; this is the way it will be." And so I began witnessing for Christ in those days. I joined the Navy back in 1939 before the war started. And then I went through the war, of course, on the USS *Yorktown*, the carrier that was bombed in the Battle of the Coral Sea, and sunk at the Battle of Midway. I was aboard the carrier when it sank. I know what war is. War is bad.

Stan Linzey Receives Baptism with the Holy Spirit

But all during that time I conducted Bible classes on the ship and men got saved. And even though, for a period of time, I did not have the baptism, many others got the baptism as I told them what it was all about. I studied concerning the baptism and finally received the baptism in a small church in West Los Angeles in 1941. I spoke in tongues for two hours and had a real filling. Now, so much for the experience! My questions were, "Now what? Is this the end? Is tongues the end of it? Can we expect anything from this? What can we expect?" This is really crucial, for some people stop at the point of receiving the baptism and don't go any further. They consider it a goal which they have attained, and that's it. It's not to be a goal at all. Rather, it is a door through which we enter in the service for the Lord Jesus Christ. Hallelujah! There shall be more experiences and life in Christ following the reception of the baptism and beyond the tongues experienced. Tongues is only the beginning of a New Testament walk, really.

And so this evening we're concerned with what happens after receiving the baptism with the Holy Spirit. We'll make three points, here. I want to discuss them with you and get our points across to you. Then I want to give you some illustrations of what's happened to people who have gotten saved and filled with the Spirit and who walk in the Spirit.

Perfection

First, Hebrew 6:1 states, "Let us go on unto perfection." Having come to Jesus Christ and having been filled with the Spirit, you are not perfect. If you were, you wouldn't need to be reading this book. But I rather doubt that you've attained perfection, so the admonition to all of us is, "Let us go on to perfection."

The baptism in the Holy Spirit is not salvation. Rather, it's a gift to those born into the family of God. Some people are saying that you have to have the baptism to be taken in the rapture. That is not scriptural at all. And some are saying you have to speak in tongues or you won't make it. That's not true at all. The baptism of the Holy Spirit is not salvation. Faith in Jesus Christ and the shed blood of Christ brings salvation. Hallelujah!

And the Scripture says that the blood of Jesus Christ, God's son, cleanses from all sin. Hallelujah! If you have placed your faith in Jesus Christ, you're saved. You're as saved as you'll ever be, for your faith is hinging on the fact of your faith in Jesus Christ. The baptism is given for powerful service, for an ability and a power to accomplish something for Jesus Christ. When you're born again, God plants within you the seed of a new nature. As Paul the Apostle said, "if any man be in Christ, he is a new creature: old things are passed away; behold, all things are become new" (II Cor. 5:17).

There is a better reading of that which will make it a little more understandable. For if you would search your hearts carefully, you probably would say to yourself, "All old things haven't passed away. All things haven't become new. Where does that leave me?" Well a better reading is, "Old things are passing away, behold, all things are becoming new." Aren't you glad it says it that way? It kind of counts us all in, doesn't it?

Motivation

And, of course, this has to do with motivation. Motivation is the basis of all of it. For if God gets hold of the motivation, He'll get a hold of the deeds and the acts that will follow. The Holy Spirit baptism opens one up to a new program—a program of power. It brings us into contact with reality and introduces us to the realities of the spiritual world. Until a person has received the baptism of the Holy Spirit, it seems he has a second-hand mind. But when he's filled with the Spirit of God, the things he knows become real to him and become a first-hand experience, and his experience is just as real and first-hand as the experiences of those disciples who received the baptism on the day of Pentecost nearly 2,000 years ago. Can you say "Amen?" That's what keeps the Christian message fresh, keeps it alive and going.

Power

According to the Greek text, Jesus said in Acts 1:8, "Ye shall receive power the Holy Ghost coming upon you. And you shall be my witnesses, both in Jerusalem and in all Judea and Samaria and unto the uttermost parts of the earth." Here is a progressive or continuing tense as the Greek text puts it, "Ye shall receive power the Holy Ghost coming upon you." That means every time He comes upon you, or as He continues to come upon you, you shall be endued with power to do the job He wants you to do. And if you pay attention to the Book of Acts, it happened just that way. The Gospel went to Judea first, and then in Acts 8 it went to Samaria, and then later on, it went to the rest of the world.

Spiritual Warfare

Being filled with the Spirit makes us become more aware of the opposing forces of good and evil. When you're filled with the Holy Spirit, you begin to be aware that there is a struggle with the spirit world, if you please. There is a struggle with the carnal nature and the spiritual forces, and this becomes very real in our lives. And we also become cognizant of the fact that we're more than conquerors through Him that loved us (Romans 8;37). We are not left to our devices. We're not left powerless and without help. Rather, He's there to take us through any strife and stress and strain and difficulties that come our way. Hallelujah! We become conscious of the presence of God. Christ becomes real.

To digress for just a moment, we would do well to do what Brother Lawrence said in his little book, *Practicing the Presence of God*. We would, indeed, do very well to practice the presence of God. In one Sunday School class, we discussed "How Can We Know Ourselves?" and "How Can We Know God?" We need to take time in meditation and reflection to practice—and that's a good term—practice the presence of God. Take time to realize that God is here, and God is with you, for after all, it is Christ in you, the hope of glory (Col. 1:27). Hallelujah!

Spirit Received at Conversion

The believer, we have found, may be filled immediately at his conversion, or he may be filled later. The sooner the better, for it does not do God any honor, does not bring glory to Jesus Christ, for a Christian to wait years and years and years to receive the baptism of the Holy Spirit. I've heard people say, "Well, God must have a reason, and He must be doing something in my life. And when He's ready, He'll fill me." That sounds so spiritual, but it just isn't true. For it's God's desire that you be filled immediately with the Holy Spirit so you'll have more years to give to Him in powerful service so that you'll do something for the Lord Jesus Christ. Hallelujah!

I've brought to your attention that everyone receives the Holy Spirit at conversion. Don't make any mistake about this. Paul said in Romans 8:9, "if any man have not the Spirit of Christ, he is none of His." So we do have the Spirit of Christ in that we've received Christ. You certainly cannot receive Him physically into your heart. You have to receive the Spirit into your heart. That is Christ. So every believer has the Holy Spirit, but that's not the infilling with the baptism in the Holy Spirit.

No Tarrying

And it is my contention that if everybody had no bias, or had not been taught contrary to the Word of God, but would be fully open to what God had to say, he would get saved and filled instantaneously, and I believe that's the New Testament pattern, and I believe we're coming back to that. We're seeing it more and more all the time. Hallelujah! It is not necessary, when one gets saved, to spend days and days in tarrying to receive the baptism in the Holy Spirit. That's not God's plan in the New Testament era. It's God's plan that you receive the gift and take it and make it yours. And nobody said, "Amen." Right? Yeah, that's right—Amen!

Now perhaps I'd better add this in here. If you want to tarry, there are certainly times to tarry. But the time to tarry is after you've come to Christ, and after you've been saved and filled with the Holy Spirit. There will be many times in your life when you'll have to wait before God, or you'll want to wait before God, while God reveals Himself to you, or deals with your character, or tries to show you something from the Word. There are many times in our lives when we have to wait before God for direction. Now this makes sense, doesn't it? And this is the way it is! But we don't wait for the infilling of the Holy Spirit, because the gift has already been given. He's not going to be given again. He has been given once for all at Pentecost, and He will be here until Jesus takes the Church out of the world. Then we'll all go with Him. Hallelujah!

On to Perfection

Now let us go on to perfection. You are not perfect now. The Lord took you as you were, and with all your faults, with all your blemishes, with all your misunderstandings, with all your failures—everything wrong with you. He saved you, and He filled you with the Holy Spirit. Now He says, "let us go on unto perfection" (Heb. 6:1). Hallelujah! One writer says at one place to let us "grow in grace, and in the knowledge of our Lord and Savior Jesus Christ" (II Peter 3:18). And you'll want to grow 'til the day you die, or 'til the day that Jesus comes for you. This is a growth process all the way down. Friends, don't come to the place where you decide you have arrived. For when you decide that, you have just failed—miserably! You haven't arrived. "Let us go on unto perfection" (Heb. 6:1).

Live in the Spirit

And the next thought is this: "If we live in the Spirit, let us also walk in the Spirit" (Galatians 5:25). Now we live in the Spirit by

God's *arrangement*. He says, "If we live in the Spirit, let us also walk in the Spirit." This living in the Spirit is by God's *arrangement*. He says, "But ye are not in the flesh, but in the Spirit, if so be that the Spirit of God dwell in you" (Rom. 8:9). This is God's *arrangement*, in which the Holy Spirit of God deals with the individual, and that person finally comes to Jesus Christ. The Holy Spirit is received at conversion. This then puts us in the realm of the Spirit. You were not in that realm before. You're in that realm now. And this is by the crucifixion principle. The Apostle Paul said, "I am crucified with Christ: nevertheless I live; yet not I, but Christ liveth in me; and the life which I now live in the flesh I live by the faith of the Son of God, who loved me, and gave Himself for me" (Gal. 2:20).

Feelings Don't Matter

Feelings don't matter. Now this is a principle. It doesn't matter how you feel about things. Feelings have nothing to do with it. The fact is, if you receive Christ, you died with Christ at Calvary. Yes, you died with Christ at Calvary, and you were raised with Christ on Easter morning. This sums up what is involved in the principle here. It doesn't matter how you feel about things. You may feel like the worst person in your town today. Well, you might be, but that has nothing to do with this. If you name the name of Jesus Christ and you're a Christian, the principle still holds.

You died with Christ, and you were raised with Christ. Hallelujah! This is not a matter of feeling at all. However, this principle should become experimental to each one of us. "I am crucified . . . nevertheless I live" (Gal. 2:20). Wait a minute! I'm crucified, but I live! I died, but Christ lives in me. What a contradiction! However, it's not confusion. It's infusion, if you please. The thought is that the apostle is so filled with Christ that he doesn't know where he stops and where Christ stops. He's all together there! It's Christ and him, intermingled. Not confusion, but interfusion. Oh hallelujah! Glory to God!

No wonder he could make a statement like that! "I am crucified . . . [yet] I live . . . not I, but Christ liveth in me" (Gal. 2:20). Hallelujah!

And so this principle should become experiential to each of us. It should be carried into the redeemed life.

Spiritual Tension

Now tension always exists between the carnal nature and the Spirit. The Scriptures indicate this if you read them carefully. Some people will seem like they never have a trouble in the world. Yet some other people seem like they're always having trouble. But I don't care who you are, if you live long enough, you're going to have difficulties sometime, somewhere, in some area. You're not going to escape them, and there's no cop-out. But where there is spiritual warfare, tension exists.

Now "we are more than conquerors, through Him that loved us" (Romans 8:37). This verse carries over into our Christian life, because we're victors in the Lord Jesus. We live in the realm of the Spirit. All actions, all desires, all our possessions, everything we have, do, or think, are now evaluated by the Spirit. The things we once thought were so wonderful, we now don't think are that way. The things we used to despise and not give much concern to, now we're finding they may be more valuable. They're evaluated by the Holy Spirit. Things of earth are measured against things eternal. Time and eternity are brought into proper perspective. We see from a different viewpoint now. Things are different with us. And this should help to get our priorities right.

Priorities

There's nothing so sad as to see a Christian having his priorities wrong. Such a person does the things that don't count, the things that are going to pass away, the things that will pass off the scene, whereas he ought to be doing the things that count for eternity, things that will be valued by God and be contributing to his treasure up there. These are the right things to be concerned about. But when Christians get priorities wrong, they're certainly in for difficulty. Note also, our bodies are temples of the Holy Spirit.

I'm amazed how little it seems that some of our people know about the Scriptures and what the Bible teaches. Furthermore, in our churches, we ought to just give a good study in church history. Every Christian ought to know church history.

Now this is not new. But you've got people who think the body is not worth anything. That's not true. They degrade it. Your bodies are temples of the Holy Spirit. Make no mistake about it. The Holy Spirit indwells your body. Don't make any mistake about it. Your body is valuable. Honey, I'm going to tell you something. If you miss the next beat, that's all you've had. If your heart don't grab the next beat, you've had it. That's all she wrote. Your body is a temple of this Holy Spirit.

This means that we ought to take care of the body. We ought not to be boozing it up; we ought not to be smoking it up; we ought not to be doing things to ruin it. Nor should we overindulge the body, either. Of course, we don't want to talk about that one. That's our favorite one. But that's the way it is. Our bodies are temples of the Holy Spirit.

So we're not to profane the temple. We're not to indulge it, either. We ought to do what we can to take care of it. However, I suppose I should add one more in here. We have people in our churches, though, who so want to take care of the body that they can't make it out to church, or Sunday School, because they've got to have that rest, you know. But when you're in the world you did everything you wanted to do. Nobody stopped you, right? I would to God we'd keep that spirit right now. Have as much vim, vigor and vitality for Jesus Christ as we had before we came to Him. The Apostle Paul to me is the epitome of this kind of teaching. He was out to wreck the Church with all the vim, vigor, vitality, and mind he had. Like somebody said, Christ had to save him, or he would have wrecked the Church. So Christ saved him and built the Church. Hallelujah! But he turned right around with the same vim, vigor, and vitality, and he used it for the glory of the Lord.

Demon Possessed Christians

And there are some people who have a thought today—people who think today that Christians can be demon-possessed, for example. That's utterly ridiculous. I don't believe that at all. I wouldn't believe that if I weren't a Pentecostal.

If that were true, what do you want to come to Jesus for? Where's your security? Where's your assurance? Where's your hope? That gives nobody any hope. If God's no stronger than the devil, why serve God? You don't even know what you're talking about, because you're making two opposing forces come into one body. You're bringing in dualism, but we refute dualism. There is only one God. And He's the Master of everything, hallelujah! And two spirits do not dwell in this temple. If the Holy Spirit indwells this temple, then the evil spirit cannot indwell the temple. Say me a good "Amen!" Hallelujah!

Being a Witness

In this realm of the Spirit, we're given to witness here below. And the paradox is, we must share the Gospel, we must share eternal life if we're going to keep our life. The Gospel is one thing you cannot keep to yourself, while keeping eternal life. You'll lose it. You've got to give it out. And the more you give out, the more you will get. This is a paradox, but this is the way it works. Jesus said it in another way: "whosoever shall lose his life for my sake and the gospel's, the same shall save it" (Mark 8:35). But if you go out to find your life, you're going to lose it, and lose your sense of bearing. You have to give it away.

"Ye shall receive power, after that the Holy Spirit is come upon you" (Acts 1:8). This is power, ability, authority, and God does give us an authority to do His work.

When one is baptized in the Holy Spirit, he arises from the altar with a new vision and motivation to win souls. And this person should be encouraged by the church to carry this out. When you're filled with the Holy Spirit, it seems to me like the desire should grip you that the next thing you want to do is win somebody to Christ. I would dare say there are Christians in your church who have never won a soul to Jesus Christ. You don't know what it is! You don't know how to turn the key, so to speak. You've wanted to, but you haven't. Something has held you back. I'll tell you what. If you ever make a believer out of somebody and bring that person to Jesus Christ, it will be just like getting a taste of blood for the first time. You can't stop any more! You've got to keep going after them and bringing them to Jesus Christ. And that's what we're supposed to do, as we're filled with the Holy Spirit. We supposed to get a new vision.

The church should encourage people. I've often wondered, and I've said this in many places, I don't know who the weakest member of the church might be. It makes no difference. All of you probably think you know who it is. And you might be wrong. You might be the one, really, but, be that as it may. If some insignificant member of the body would stand and rise and say, "Brother, I feel like God has asked me to go down to Main Street, and He wants me to preach on the street corner." Do you know what the church would probably say? "Oh is that so? Where did you get that wild idea?" That's what would happen, whereas the church ought to rise up as one person and say, "God bless you! Let's lay hands on you! I hope you can do it." That ought to be the attitude. But we're the greatest bunch of negative thinkers sometimes, aren't we?

We "know" all the reasons why it can't be done. Therefore, that's why it doesn't get done. Well I say, "God bless you, go to it, and I hope you can make it." And it wouldn't be a bad idea if somebody would say, "If you'll go, I'll go with you. We'll see if the two of us can do it." Oh, God give us people with vision! Give us people with a vision to want to do something! I don't care what it looks like! Just go do something! I would rather do something and make a miserable failure than to play it safe and never do anything. You've got a bunch of people always playing it safe. You'll never catch them between second and third; they're always playing it safe. I like the guy who gets caught in the middle. Brother, he's got to do something. And it's fun to watch him do it. But, generally, those kind make it. And God gets the glory, and souls get saved. But some wonder, "How come?"

I had somebody say to me the other day, "Of all the experiences, where do you get all the experiences you talk about?" I said, "I have them. It's better than reading about them." Hallelujah! I don't buy the books and put them on my shelf and read who did what, where. I go out and have experiences myself. It's more fun that way. Hallelujah! And then when something happens, you don't forget it. And sometimes it gets tough. Then you scamper for the base and see if you can make it. Sometimes you don't, and you fall flat on your face. So what? That doesn't hurt anybody. Just get up and go again, that's all.

When you are filled with the Spirit, there's power for salvation. There's power for healing. There's esteem for the Word of God. We are now living in the realm of the Spirit. And the spiritual thirst is quenched by the living waters, and Christ is made real to the hearts of His people. And so let us go on to perfection, and then let us live in the Spirit.

Walk in the Spirit

Now the next point is this: let us walk in the Spirit. Now I brought it to your attention that when Galatians 5:25 says, "If we live in the Spirit," it also says "let us also walk in the Spirit." This has to do with motivation. This is by God's *arrangement*, not ours. God initiates the action. And we come to Christ. We're saved and brought into the spiritual realm. Now where it says, "let us walk in the Spirit," this is by our own *volition*, if you please. In other words, this is something I must do about it. God did His part. He brought me into the spiritual realm. That's one thing. Now my *volition* is to walk in the Spirit.

When I used to read that some years ago, I would say, "Well, if you *live* in the Spirit, you're bound to have to *walk* in the Spirit." That's not true. There are many Christians today who don't *live* and don't *walk* in the Spirit. They're in the spiritual realm, but they're doing the things of the flesh. And it names them here. I'm not going to go over all of them, but we read them in the fifth chapter of Galatians. These are the works of the flesh from Christians who ought to know better. No. Our own volition is to *walk* in the Spirit. Paul's crucifixion of the flesh is not an end in itself, but is the removal of the roadblock on the royal highway to freedom. And here, I must be honest with you, in this Scripture he is refuting legalism. He is against legalism in any form. And we Christians are not to be legalists in any form. It's amazing how some people want all kinds of rules laid out. You know, "You can't do this, you don't do this, and you don't do that!" It's rules, rules, rules! My friend, if you live in the Spirit and walk in the Spirit, it's not a lot of rules. It's about serving God because you love Jesus Christ, and you'll fulfill the royal law. Hallelujah! Glory to God!

In Galatians 5:25, Paul says, "If we live in the Spirit, let us also walk in the Spirit." Now notice this word *walk*—there are two terms given for the word *walk*. I'm going to bring them to your attention.

In this case, the word *walk* is the Greek word *stoicomen*, which means, "let us walk in line," "let us walk in step," and "let us walk in fellowship." This has to do with motives, for motives are stressed by this word. Yet, it's our own *volition*. One must live his life in accordance with the mind of Christ. And again, here is a principle. Sometimes we are very uncritical in the way we read the Scriptures. We don't understand, or we don't take time to understand. One principle is to have the mind of Christ. Yet, we're responsible for our own actions.

Now I suppose a lot of you have read Charles Sheldon's book, *In His Steps*—a very wonderful book. It's a classic. Except it just doesn't work. That's the only trouble with it. For Sheldon's thesis is that when you get in a tight spot, all you do is you ask the question, "What would Jesus do if He were in my place?"

What Would Jesus Do?

Quite honestly, I have been in places where I cannot imagine Jesus ever being. And I don't know what He would do. I can't ask that kind of a question, because I can't get an answer. For example, I was in the military. I was in the United States Navy. What would Jesus do if He were in the Navy? I don't know. There was no Navy in Jesus' day. Jesus did not belong to the military. He was not in the Roman Army. I don't know what He would have done in the Army. So the question is not, "What would Jesus do?" The question rather is, "What would Jesus have me do?" There's the question. And that's what I have to decide once in a while. I have to make decisions once in a while, and I want to tell you that it's not always easy. Sometimes, if the questions always required a black or white decision, we wouldn't have any trouble, would we? But I don't know about you. When the questions come to me, the decisions are generally the various shades of gray. And I have to decide, "Which one's the whitest?" I don't know. But what would Jesus have me do? And we're talking about the mind of Christ.

The Mind of Christ

Decisions are ours. Now when we become Christians, our minds are not supplanted. Now people don't say this and this may sound ridiculous. But some Christians get the idea that when they get the mind of Christ, they think the Lord just took the top of their heads off and took their brains out. And I don't know what He put in. But they're going to try to operate from there, and it's pretty difficult. But that's not the idea here at all. We still have our own minds. And yet we've got to make decisions based on the mind of Christ.

Paul had to determine the requirements of the moment. We have to grow up and mature, and this is tough. Jesus does not take our minds away. You know, we Christians get double-minded. We don't say this, but I've had to analyze this. What is it to be led by the Spirit? You know, that's kind of a tough question. Well, we get the idea that the Lord is standing right by our side. And I guess if you get in a tough spot you just say, "Hey Jesus, what do I do now?" And I guess He talks in your head and tells you. I don't know. That has not been my experience. But that's the way it sounds like some people act.

That's not the way it is at all. Rather, the Holy Spirit moves in and operates in and through your mind. You're not a double-minded individual, or you shouldn't be. You should be an integrated mind, an integrated individual, if you please, so that when you think, you think the thoughts of God.

For example, some years ago, I pastored a church in El Cajon, California. And I just built the church. We had just bought opera chairs from a theater and put them in. And I had some chairs left over. Well you don't want to keep any extra chairs around. You would rather give them to another church if you can, after you keep a few spare parts. And so one day I said to my wife, "Let's go to Calexico." Calexico is a border town, south of El Centro, California. I had no reason to go to Calexico. I didn't know anybody in Calexico. But somehow, I wanted to go to Calexico.

She said, "What for?"

I said, "I don't know."

She said, "Okay."

So we got in the car, and we went to Calexico. We got there just about noon and drove by the Assembly of God church. Well, just about noon, I said, "Let's stop by. They're probably eating. We'll just eat with them." That to me sounded like a pretty good idea.

And so we stopped by and met the pastor down there. And they were eating. I had guessed rightly. And so we stopped. "Won't you have lunch?"

"I thought you'd never ask." And so, we had lunch with them.

And afterward he was showing me around in his church. They had just bought a new organ. He's showing me all of that, and he had real benches. Now, I hadn't been thinking about chairs. And he made the statement, "We're going to buy chairs."

I said, "Chairs? I'll sell you chairs."

"How many?" he asked.

I told him.

"What do you want?" he asked.

I said, "Two dollars apiece."

He said, "I'll take them."

I said, "Write me a check."

The business was over. And right then, I was ready to go home. Business had been taken care of. But that's being led by the Spirit. God works in and through our minds to accomplish things for His own glory. Hallelujah!

Spiritual Maturity

We have to grow up and mature and be responsible for our decisions, however. Christ was the foundation of the temple of the Spirit, but Paul and his fellow Christians had to make the blueprints and specifications and furnish the materials and labor for the superstructure. Jesus Christ gave the guidelines. Now you have to work it out from that point. That will make you grow up fast if you live through it. But that's what you have to do. But legalists want a building code, with all the plans and all the decisions laid down in black and white. They want the rules down so nobody makes a mistake. I'll tell you what, honey. If you're going to live for Jesus Christ, you have to run the risk of mistakes. But you have to be man enough and woman enough to stand up for your mistakes and admit mistakes and say, "Yes, I goofed, Lord, forgive me." But He forgives you just that quick and keeps you going on. Hallelujah. But you learn to be mature. That's what it's all about.

Legalism

Sometimes we have trouble in our churches because of legalism—what rules this, this, and this. Christ does not give rules. There's just a few rules, and if you notice who the law is for, read it in I Timothy. It's for the terrible transgressors. That's who the law is for. The law is not for people who are living in the Spirit and trying to serve Jesus Christ. Say me a good "Amen." Hallelujah!

Walking in the Spirit

In Galatians 5:16, we have the term, *walk,* again. It says, "Walk in the Spirit, and ye shall not fulfill the lust of the flesh." Now the term *walk* here is another word. It is not the same word as *walk* that we discussed a few moments ago. This word, *peripatete,* has to do with holiness, cleanliness, right conduct, and ethics. We are short on ethics in some places, I'll tell you for sure. We're short on right conduct in some places, I'll tell you for sure. It's too bad when you have more regard for a worldly businessman than you do a Christian. But sometimes the world has better ethics and better conduct in business than some of us do. That's a shame, and that's a disgrace. My friend, if we're going to be God's people, let's see to it that our conduct and our ethics are right, irreproachable, and unblameable, if you please. Hallelujah!

This should flow from the motivation. This *walk* should flow from the other *walk,* which has to do with motivation. However, reminders are needed. And then Paul the Apostle states in Galatians 5:18, "if ye be led of the Spirit, ye are not under the law." And we discussed the fact of leadership of the Spirit. But sometimes we get confused here. How can I know I can be led by the Spirit? What is it to be led by the Spirit? Sometimes we don't know. Once, when I was in Bakersfield, California, I had been invited down on a Sunday to minister on the Holy Spirit. And as I do elsewhere, we provided a time for questions and answers. And so the question came up, "How do you know you're led by the Spirit?" Or, "How can you be led by the Spirit?" And I thought for a few moments and finally I said, "Well, I guess we can put it this way—what the world calls hunches, if we were smart enough, we'd have them too. Only, the source is the Holy Spirit. If we would follow the hunches that God gives us, we would walk in the Spirit. And the pastor said, "I'm so glad you used that term, *hunches*. We understand that. We know what that means." Otherwise, when we talk of being by the Spirit, many of us do not know what it means.

Witnessing

Down south some months ago, a great number of our family members were together. And, of course, when you get my family together, as big as my family is, you're bound to have discussions on nearly anything you want to talk about. And sometimes it gets rather vociferous, because they all have very high opinions of what they think. Most of them take after their dad, and what is right is right. And that's the way it goes.

But now Verna Linzey thinks that's funny, because she knows who's turning their heads in this family, after all. But some of the young men were discussing being led of the Spirit and how to be led by the Spirit. Finally, one of my sons-in-law, who's a Georgia cracker, and just has plenty of common sense, said, "Well, I'm going to tell you what it is to be led by the Spirit. You do what's supposed to be done. That's what you do." Well, you can't argue with that one, can you? If something's got to be done, that's what you do. That's being led by the Spirit. Duty and responsibility call for appropriate action! Use your heads! It's not all glorious. Sometimes decisions have to be made. And so, we are led by the Spirit by the little nudges and the hunches that the Holy Spirit gives us. If you would learn to go by some of these things, you would find a great adventuresome walk in the Spirit. And pretty soon you'll begin to learn what is God and what is not God, if you're observant and careful. You will begin to learn how to walk in the Spirit. Hallelujah!

One of my daughters one time told me something, and I think it was great. She said she was at home and all cooped up and wanted to get out. And so, finally, she said, "I'm just going to go outside. I'm going to go to some apartment and knock on a door and see if I can lead somebody to Christ. She had made up her mind to do it. So she got up, put on her snow clothes, and went out, and knocked on a door. And here, a guy answers the door. She went in and talked to the guy and he gets converted. They now belong to the church. That's being led of the Spirit. Having some "get up and go" and some gumption and not being afraid. Right? Yes. Quit playing it safe. See what will happen. It's more fun that way. Hallelujah!

We need to get the mind of Christ and live in the realm of the Spirit. That's God's *action* and God's *arrangement*. And then the daily *walk* in the Spirit—that's our *volitional* following what God would have us do. And then the mind of Christ and our mind become one.

CONCLUSION

In conclusion, after tongues, we must go on to perfection. You have not arrived. You haven't got it all. There's still much more to get. Still a lot more to learn. Still a lot more right conduct to practice. Let's go on to perfection. And then we must live in the Spirit—that is, we must learn to operate in that realm of the Spirit that God has placed us in, leaving the things of the flesh and carnality behind, learning the tension that exists, and yet having victory in Christ to live for the Lord Jesus Christ. Then we must walk in the Spirit. This has to do with our volition. *I want to walk in the Spirit. I will to walk in the Spirit*, because of what Christ has done for me. And in doing that, we do what is at hand. As the Scriptures declare, "Whatsoever ye do, do it heartily, as to the Lord, and not unto men" (Colossians 3:23). Put everything you've got to it.

Friends, this life is passing us by pretty quickly. You older people know what I'm talking about. Time is getting away. What you're going to do for Jesus Christ, you're going to pretty well have to do as fast as you can do it. Time will get away. You can't go back and undo. You can't go back and say, "If I had one more chance." No, those are gone forever. What you're going to do, you've got to do now. You've got to make time count now.

Sometimes, in my thinking, I place myself in eternity and try to picture what it will be like there. And I see the scene of those who've really gone out, like Paul the Apostle, like the disciples, like others whom we've known in Church history. They have given everything. I see what's happening up there. Then I see maybe myself or some others. We've kind of fiddled along a little bit. We haven't been too serious. We haven't gone out all the way, and we think, "God, if I had one more chance, there are some things I'd do that I haven't been doing. There are some things I have been doing I wouldn't do, if I had this chance again." Friends, you haven't got it. No, you haven't got it. When time passes you by, that's all for that time. And so we've got to plan and do what is at hand.

I previously mentioned that I was in Bakersfield, California, recently. God gave us a good meeting. Oh, it was a beautiful meeting. In that one service, about 16 received the Holy Spirit in one night. We had a grand time. I'll never forget Brother and Sister H.B. Garlock, our retired missionaries to Africa, who belong to that church. And during the service, Sister Garlock got so tickled. She laughed out loud and broke the church up. And we had a grand time, I'll tell you for sure.

Babsom College

But after tongues, what? The question was asked. And this thought came to my mind. I have a letter in my hand that I received from a Brother Bunk, who was in Babsom College, Wellesley, Massachusetts. He belonged to the Assembly of God church in Springfield, Massachusetts, one of our finest churches on the East Coast in southern New England. Pastor Ed Burkey was the pastor. I got this letter in November 1973. He stated,

> Dear Chaplain, you undoubtedly have met and ministered to hundreds of young people during the past three years, so you probably do not recall having met me. I am a member of Bethany Assembly of God Church in Springfield, Massachusetts. Edward B. Burkey is the pastor. And about three years ago on December 7, 1970, to be exact, you preached at our church about the baptism with the Holy Spirit. After the evening service, we held what you called a Holy Spirit clinic, where those who wanted the

filling of the Holy Spirit could be prayed for. I had accepted the Lord Jesus Christ in the spring of 1970, and at the time you came to Bethany, I had not yet received the baptism. So I was among the patients at the clinic. The Lord filled me with His wonderful Spirit that night when you laid hands on me. Praise the Lord! I am now in my junior year at Babsom College in Wellesley, Massachusetts, where I am working on a Bachelor of Science degree in business administration with a major in management and organizational behavior. I will graduate in May of 1975. The Lord has blessed me and used me in at least one special way during my past two-and-a-half years at Babsom, and that is in the founding of the Babsom Christian Fellowship. I am the president of the Fellowship this year—an evangelical student organization which is now a chapter of intervarsity Christian fellowship. The Fellowship has grown and developed during the past two-and-a-half years from a small, obscure group of Babsom students, to the most respected and active organization on campus. The Holy Spirit has moved, and He's continued to move through the members of the group to bring glory to the Lord Jesus Christ.

After tongues, what? He went on to do something for Christ— to go to college, to form the Babsom Christian Fellowship, where other people find Christ and are filled with the Spirit. This is what you do! This is how you go serve Him.

Naval Air Station Moffett Field

Here is another illustration I want to bring to your attention— to me, one of the most touching I've had. I was the Staff Chaplain at Naval Air Station Moffett Field in 1973 to 1974, which means I was also on the Admiral's staff. This also means that I had the right to go to any squadron in the fleet, wherever they might be, as the Staff Chaplain.

In 1973, I was invited to speak and give an orientation lecture to one of the squadrons, which I did. So I went over there. I got there just a little bit early. And when I arrived, the leading chief of the squadron met me. Now he was a veteran chief. This guy had been a hard liver[13] for several years. He met me and told me who he was, and said, "You're a little bit early, Chaplain. Come on in. We'll have a cup of coffee. And when the time comes, I will introduce you." This old chief had 23 years in the Navy. And so, as we sat and drank coffee and as we talked, the subject of religion came up.

I said, "Well, what church do you belong to or do you go to?"

He mentioned that he attended a Full Gospel Church in Concord, California. He said, "I go to the Pentecostal Church of God."

I said, "Well Chief, have you received the baptism in the Holy Spirit?"

And he brightened up and said, "No, I haven't. But I'm seeking it."

I said, "Chief, I've got just the thing for you. I'm the guy you need to know."

He said, "Is that right?"

I said, "That's right. You can receive it in a minute."

He said, "Really?"

I said, "Really!"

And he said, "I'm going to go to your office after this and I'm going to get it."

I said, "You be my guest."

And so after my lecture to the squadron, he followed me over to my office. He had accepted the Lord just a little time before that time. I took the Scriptures out and explained them to him. I said, "Chief, since you've accepted Jesus Christ, you already have the Holy Spirit."

He said, "That makes sense to me."

And I said, "Since you've got the Holy Spirit, when I lay hands on you, all you've got to do is open your mouth and talk in tongues." And I talked to him a little bit longer. I said, "Do you understand this?"

He said, "This is the most sense I've ever heard. In my church; they don't even talk sense, and they wonder why I don't get it."

So I said, "Okay, Chief, here we go. I'm going to lay hands on you. Get ready!" And boy, his eyes were gleaming about now—this old Chief. I laid hands on this Chief, and I was talking to him. I said, "God, fill him with the Holy Ghost." That old Chief raised both hands and began talking in tongues a little bit. All of a sudden, the thing caught fire. And boy, off he was going! Talking in tongues and having a beautiful time! Hallelujah! And so that was wonderful. I said, "Go home and tell your wife."

Now this is the odd thing. The wife had been going to church alone then. She was a "goody-goody." You know what I mean? The "goody-goodies" have trouble getting things because they're so good. The bad people know they need it, so they get it. His wife had always gone to church. She didn't have the baptism. So he went home and told her. I spoke later at a district men's fellowship in northern California. And I thought I'd touch down with the old Chief again and see how things were going, so I could tell the men's fellowship.

So I got a hold of the Chief and I said, "Hey Chief, how are things going? How do you feel?"

He said, "Oh, I feel great! Feel wonderful. When you laid hands on me, I did as you suggested. I took a word from you and spoke. Then it came. I could speak by myself. I had good feelings and I remember smiling about what had happened. I had joy, unexplainable. I could hardly wait to get home and tell my wife. Neither she nor the children have the baptism. Not only that, but they don't always go to church like they should."

I said, "Well, Chief, what did she say?"

She said, "I don't believe it. How come you can get it? You haven't even been saved very long. Anyway, you're probably the same old 'gotcha' fellow anyway."

And then he began to witness to new converts in his Sunday School. He said, "Now, Chaplain, I can talk in tongues any time I want to."

I said, "That's right, Chief, you can."

He said, "It gets easier and easier."

I said, "That's right, Chief, it does. The more you practice, the easier it gets."

He said, "I feel closer to God."

When you finally get in the move of the Spirit, things begin to happen. If you'll just take a step and do something, things begin to happen. Now, remember, this fellow had been rough. Before he got saved, he'd been a boozer, a drunk. I mean, you name it, he did it. He was a real man if you want to say it that way. But after receiving the baptism with the Holy Spirit, he began to have an exciting life. Then there came a new experience to the Chief. He said, "Chaplain, let me tell you something." He explained that he had a diabetic father. His father's leg had recently swelled so much so that it had pulled his ankle bone out of joint. That's how serious it was. They hauled him to the hospital immediately. And the Chief spoke to his pastor, and they both prayed for the father. Then the Chief said, "I felt like God wanted me to go pray for my father." So the Chief took leave from the Navy and went to his father's bedside at the hospital, somewhere up in Oregon. This was on a Wednesday.

Now listen to this. I think this is the greatest mark of humility I have heard in a long time. His father knew what his son had been. He went to his father's bedside, and his dad looked at him. He told his father, "Dad, this may seem strange to you, that your number one evil son has come to pray for you." Oh, hallelujah! Isn't that something? "Your number one evil son has come to pray for you." The Chief said, "But I had to do it." Then he read to his father from the parable of the cursed fig tree. Jesus said that anyone could have whatever he asked for if he believed. He said, "Chaplain, that's a big word."

I said, "Yes, it is, Chief."

And then when he read from Mark 16, he told his father that God would heal him. And then he asked his father if he believed it. His father said that he did. Then the Chief laid hands on him and prayed. He said, "A year ago, I would have been down to the bar somewhere. Now, I have someone who's stronger than whiskey."

He prayed for his father on a Wednesday. On the following Friday, the doctor called and told him to come and take his father home. The swelling was going out of his leg. At the last time I talked to the Chief, the dad had not fully recovered yet, but it looked good. Hallelujah!

And then, a little bit later than that, for the first time, the whole family went to church together, which they had not done before—He and his wife and three children. God had made a change in this Navy man's life. God had saved him and brought him into the realm of the Spirit. Then the Chief got filled with the Holy Ghost and began to walk in the Spirit. Hallelujah! And the last thing I heard, the Chief said, "I've got a lot of growing to do."

I said, "That's right, we do."

But from here on, we grow in grace and knowledge of the Lord and Savior Jesus Christ.

My friends, this is the way it is. We grow after we get saved and get filled. We begin to serve God and to walk in the Spirit as we've been brought into the realm of the Spirit.

May God bless these few thoughts to our hearts and minds.

Benediction

Heavenly Father, we thank you for your goodness to us and your mercies that have been extended to us. You've brought us into the realm of the Spirit by regeneration. Now, Lord, help us to walk in the Spirit by our own volition and leading of the Spirit. Bless this people. Encourage this people. Stir this people to greater things, to the conversion of their cities, oh God. Fill everyone with the Holy Ghost. Impart power for service, and Lord may the fruit of the Spirit be evident in each life, that they will love one another and love You, and love the sinner outside the gate, that others may be brought in. This we pray in Jesus' name. Amen.

NOTES

1   "Ablution" means "cleansing," "washing" (p. 2)

2   "Endued" means "to be given power" or "have power put upon one" (p.5)

3   "Tarrying" means simply to "wait" (p. 6)

4   "Fall down" while praying is often called "slain in the Spirit" (p. 22)

5   "Flesh," as opposed to being "led by the Spirit" (p. 68)

6   "Manifest" is to "show" or "display" (p. 90)

7   "Bugaboos" are "scary things" (p. 97)

8   "Holy War" is the same as the Seven Day War (p. 99)

9   "Christ Ambassador rally" is the name given to Assemblies of God youth rallies (p. 102)

10 "Bobbed" hair is "short" hair, considered unacceptable by some Holiness Pentecostals (p. 108)

11 Sandia Base was the principle nuclear weapons installation of the U. S. Department of Defense from 1946 to 1971 (p. 125)

12 "Autovon" was the military phone system (p. 129)

13 "Hard liver" is one who lives wildly, without restraint (p. 158)

RECOMMENDED READING
BY VERNA M. LINZEY, D.D.

Barclay, William. *The Promise of the Spirit*. Philadelphia: Westminster Press, 1976.

Basham, Don. *A Handbook on the Holy Spirit*. Monroeville, PA: Whitaker Books, 1969.

Bennett, Dennis. *Nine O' Clock in the Morning*, Plainfield, New Jersey: Logos International, 1970.

Blumhofer, Edith L. *Pentecost in My Soul*. Springfield, MO: Gospel Publishing House, 1970.

Boyd, Frank M. *The Spirit Works Today*. Springfield, MO: Gospel Publishing House, 1970.

Brandt, R.L. *"The Case for Speaking with Other Tongues,"* Pentecostal Evangel, 48 (June 5, 1960): 4.

Bright, Bill. *The Holy Spirit: the Key to Supernatural Living*. San Bernardino, CA: Here's Life Publishers, Inc. 1980.

Bruner, Frederick Dale. *A Theology of the Holy Spirit: The Pentecostal Experience and the New Testament Witness*. Grand Rapids: Wm. B. Eerdmans Pub., 1970.

Christiansen, Larry. *Speaking In Tongues and its Significance for the Church*. London: Fountain Trust, 1968.

Conner, Walter Thomas. *The Work of the Holy Spirit: A Treatment of the Biblical Doctrine of Divine Spirit*. Nashville: Broadman Press, 1949.

Duffield, Guy P. and Nathaniel M. Van Cleave. *Foundation of Pentecostal Theology*. Los Angeles: L.I.F.E. Bible College, 1983.

Du Plessis, David. *The Spirit Bade Me Go*. Plainfield, NJ: Logos International, 1970.

Durasoff, Steve. *Bright Wind of the Spirit: Pentecostalism Today*. Tulsa, OK: RHEMA Bible Church, 1972.

Ellis, F.M. "*The Holy Spirit and the Christian,*" *The Person and Ministry of the Holy Spirit*, ed. A.C. Dixon. New York: Garland Pub. Inc., 45 vols., 1880-1950.

Frost, Robert C. *Overflowing Life*. Plainfield, NJ: Logos International, 1971.

Frost, Robert C. *Set My Spirit Free*. Plainfield, NJ: Logos International, 1973.

Gee, Donald. *All with One Accord*. Springfield, MO: Gospel Publishing House, 1961.

Heron, Alasdair I. C. *The Holy Spirit*. Philadelphia: Westminster Press, 1983.

Hollenweger, Walter J. *The Pentecostals*. Peabody, Mass: Henrickson Publishers, 1972.

Horton, Harold. *The Gifts of the Holy Spirit*. 5th ed. Springfield, MO: Gospel Publishing House, 1953.

Humphries, A. L. *The Holy Spirit in Faith and Experience*.

Hunter, Charles and Frances. *Two Sides of a Coin*. Old Tappan, NJ: Fleming H. Revell Co., 1973.

Jorstad, Erling, Ed. *The Holy Spirit in Today's Church: A Handbook of the New Pentecostalism*. New York: Abingdon Press, 1973.

Kelsey, Morton. *Tongues Speaking: An Experiment in Spiritual Experience*. New York: Crossroad, 1964.

Linzey, James F. *A Divine Appointment in Washington, D.C.* Lafayette, LA: Huntington House Publishers, 1999.

Linzey, James F. *The Holy Spirit*. Fairfax, VA: Xulon Press, 2004.

Linzey, Verna M. *Spirit Baptism*. Fairfax, VA: Xulon Press, 2009.

Linzey, Verna M. *The Baptism with the Holy Spirit*. Fairfax, VA: Xulon Press, 2005.

McEntire, James R. *The Life of the Holy Spirit*. St. Louis, MO: Bethany Press, 1930.

Military Chaplains. *The Leader's Bible*.

Mooth, Verla A. *The Age of the Spirit*. Pecos: Dove Publications, 1972.

Nelson, P.C. *The Baptism in the Spirit*. Enid, OK: Southwestern, 1972.

Otis, George. *High Adventure*. Old Tappan, NJ: Fleming H. Revell Co, 1971.

Pache, Rene. *The Person and Work of the Holy Spirit*. Trans. J. D. Emerson. Chicago: Moody Press, 1954.

Pearlman, Myer. *Knowing the Doctrines of the Bible*. Springfield, MO: Gospel Publishing House, 1939.

Pulkington, Graham. *Gathered for Power*. New York: Morehouse-Barlow Co, 1972.

Ranaghan, Kevin and Dorothy. *Catholic Pentecostals Today*. South Bend, Indiana: Charismatic Renewal Services, 1983.

Riggs, Ralph. *The Spirit Himself.* Springfield, MO: Gospel Publishing House, 1949.

Ryrie, Charles Caldwell. *The Holy Spirit.* Chicago: Moody Bible Institute, 1965.

Schlep, John A. *Baptism in the Spirit According to Scripture.* Plainfield, NJ: Logos International, 1972.

Sherrill, John R. *They Speak with Other Tongues.* New York: McGraw-Hill, 1964.

Stott, John R. W. *Baptism and Fullness of the Holy Spirit.* Downer's Grove, ILL.: Intervarsity Press, 1964.

Sweet, Henry Barclay. *The Holy Spirit in the New Testament.* Grand Rapids: Baker Book House (c. 1910), 1976.

Thomas, W. H. Griffith. *The Holy Spirit of God.* Grand Rapids: Erdmann's 1972.

Torrey, R.A. *The Baptism with the Holy Spirit.* Minneapolis, MN: Dimension Books, 1972.

APPENDIX A

How General Ralph E. Haines, Jr., USA (CONARC) Received the Baptism with the Holy Spirit

by Colonel Myrl Allinder, USMC-Ret.

Here is what happened in Buffalo, New York, in July 1971, with General Ralph E. Haines, Jr., US Army (CONARC).

Chester (Chet) Wyrich, a Full Gospel Business Men's Fellowship, International business man from Buffalo, New York, organized a small convention at a hotel and somehow obtained General Ralph Haines as the speaker for a Saturday morning Military Prayer Breakfast. Commander Carl Wilgus, USN, had begun military prayer breakfasts in the Bureau of Naval Personnel (BUPERS) Admiral's dining room in 1967; and military prayer breakfasts were catching on.

General Haines was the last CONARC (Continental Army Commander). General George Washington was the first CONARC. General Haines commanded all Army Bases in the Continental USA with over 1,000,000 soldiers. Chet invited me to come along to Buffalo as a sort of aide for General Haines, who arrived by military air on Friday afternoon before he was to speak Saturday morning. When General Haines first stepped off the aircraft, he looked weary and worn, and all I could think was "dead." His face looked wrinkled as a prune.

General Haines was persuaded to have supper with us at the Friday evening meeting, where the Lutheran priest, Harald Bredesen, was to speak. I sat on General Haines' left at the head table. Pat Robertson was present. And instead of speaking, Pastor Bredesen asked us to stand and sing "There's a Sweet Spirit in This Place." As we stood and began to sing, General Haines began to tremble! And I positioned myself to catch him, because I thought he may be having a heart attack and dying. Instead, General Haines' arms shot straight up in the air! Light blazed from his face, knocking over people from their tables! General Haines began to shout in another language, as his face became smooth as a baby's, with light radiating from him!

The whole hotel was stirred all Friday night. When General Haines stood to speak at the Military Prayer Breakfast the next morning, he tore up his previously scripted "dry weather report," and made an astounding statement: "I don't know what Jesus is telling me to do, but whatever it is, I am going to do it!"

General Haines then began to visit every Army Base in America. He would gather all the officers in the Base Chapel, to read to them from the General Orders as first laid down by General George Washington, which state: "The Commanding Officer is responsible for the SPIRITUAL LEADERSHIP [my emphasis] of his soldiers." General Haines stated, "Gentlemen, if you are going to be a spiritual leader, you need a spiritual experience. Now let me tell you about mine." He would then confess his salvation and Baptism in the Holy Spirit! He concluded by adding, "It is better to be a private in the Army of Jesus than to be a general in the Army of America."

Therefore, General Haines began to be denounced throughout America, culminating in Senator Jacob Javits of NY denouncing Haines on the floor of the Senate (and in the pages of the *Washington Post*, *NY Times*, and other papers), and finally General Haines' relief as CONARC under President Nixon. But the testimony of the 98 year old "private in the Army of Jesus Christ" continues to echo through the Army and on the front page of a recent 2010 *Army Times*.

Editorial Note:

Some time after receiving the baptism with the Holy Spirit, General Haines was believed to have been responsible for Chaplain Jim Ammerman forming Chaplaincy of Full Gospel Churches, to endorse Spirit-filled ministers for the military chaplaincy. Captain Stanford Linzey and his son, Chaplain (MAJOR) Jim Linzey, USAR (Ret.), who was endorsed by Colonel Ammerman, spoke for some of their conventions.

APPENDIX B

How to Help Others Receive
the Baptism in the Spirit

by Chaplain (MAJOR), James F. Linzey, ARNG (Ret.)

1. Open in prayer. Explain that the baptism with the Holy Spirit is *the reception of the Holy Spirit as confirmed by speaking in tongues*. All Christians have received the Holy Spirit at salvation according to Romans 8:9. The question then is, "Have you confirmed it through speaking in tongues?" This is a privilege of every believer for each one has received the Holy Spirit. This "session" is to confirm that they have received the Holy Spirit through speaking in tongues.

2. Share and expound on these Scriptures: Joel 2:28-29; Matt. 3:11; Luke 24:49; John 7:37-39; Acts 1:8, 2:1-18, 2:38-39, 8:14-17, 10:44-46, 19:1-7; Rom. 8:9; I Cor. 6:19, 12:13, 14:10, 14-15, and 18.

3. Emphasize that "the promise is unto you, and to your children, and to all that are afar off…" (Acts 2:39).

4. Inform the believers that they are going to manifest the indwelling Holy Spirit as you and other Spirit-filled believers begin to pray in tongues, not in their native language.

5. Tell them to speak out by faith, for the Holy Spirit will give them utterance. Emphasize that every utterance has meaning with God, according to I Cor. 14:10 which says, "There are, perhaps, a great many kinds of languages in the world, and no kind is without meaning" (NASB). So it's impossible to make a mistake. The diverse tongues at Babel in Gen. 11:7-9 separated man, but the reception of the Holy Spirit *as confirmed* with the speaking of diverse tongues at Pentecost in Acts 2:4, and since then, unifies man.

6. Explain that when you lay your hand on their heads, they are to enter in with you and pray in tongues at that moment. Remind them that they must do the speaking as Paul the Apostle taught in I Cor. 14:14-15 and 18.

7. After believers speak in tongues, encourage them to do so daily. Do not put a guilt trip on those who do not speak in tongues. Encourage them to speak out by faith in their private prayer closet or offer to pray with them in the future when they are more ready to take this step of faith. Close in prayer.

Appendix C
Military Prayers

A Prayer for the United States Air Force

Heavenly Father, Lord and Savior of us all, we come before You beseeching Your Divine protection over the Air Force as we embark upon our missions. We honor You as our Guide and Comforter as You lead us by Your Spirit day by day. Enable us, Lord, to use the skills and knowledge we have been trained to use to fulfill the charges our rank or station requires of us. Continue to give guidance and wisdom to our Airmen in the fulfillment of the orders and duties they have sworn to carry out. We thank you for your mantle of love over our families whom we trust to your care and guidance that they may live in safety, health, and peace. Protect them from the enemy of our souls as You sustain them with Your love. Strengthen all of us by Your Holy Spirit in all that we do in service to America and the United States Air Force as we are careful to give you the praise, the glory, and our devotion in humble obedience to Your commands as you sustain us by Your blessed Spirit. In Christ Jesus' name we pray. Amen.

– Chaplain, Lieutenant Colonel Jack J. Chinn, USAF (Ret.)

A PRAYER FOR THE UNITED STATES ARMY

Almighty God, we earnestly ask that, out of your loving and tender mercies, you would place within the minds of your Soldiers the knowledge to do your will in times of war and in times of peace. Graciously impart to your Soldiers the wisdom to discern your will, O Lord, and the moral courage to implement your will in their daily lives. Lead your Soldiers to call upon you so that by your power they may advance from victory to victory, crushing the oppression of wickedness that would otherwise defeat them. And we ask that you would use the Army as one of your righteous tools to establish your justice throughout the world. Through Jesus Christ our Lord we pray. Amen.

– Chaplain (MAJOR) James F. Linzey, USAR (Ret.)

A Prayer for the United States Coast Guard

Almighty God, Maker of heaven and earth, by Your will are set the boundaries of the nations. Grant to the men and women who guard our shores that selfless devotion that is woven into the very fabric of Coast Guard tradition. Give to them the skill, wisdom and seamanship that will enable them to thwart every attempt to flood our coasts with contraband, illegal drugs or evil terrorists. In lonely nights as they stand watch, sustain them with your presence. Protect them, O Lord, as they risk their lives to save the lives of others. And when they have weathered life's last storm may they find safe haven in the love of Him who calmed the raging sea and gave His life to save all who trust Him. Through Jesus Christ our Lord we pray. Amen.

– Commander R. Glen Brown, CHC, USN, (Ret.)

A Prayer for The United States Marine Corps

Heavenly Father, we lift to you the men and women of the Marine Corps; hold them in your loving hands, protecting them as they protect us. Keep their bodies in your care; keep their hearts true to the ideals of the Corps and the precepts of your Word; keep their minds clear and focused on the task at hand. Reveal your presence and love to them in every situation in life. When at leisure, may they wish to please you; when in harm's way, let them sense your guidance; when wounded or afraid, let them know your comfort; when showing kindness to those in need or to children, may they do it in the knowledge of your approval; and be their Saviour to the end of their life and beyond. God bless and protect the Corps as she serves the United States of America. May her cause ever be righteous, and may it be pursued with a true and gallant heart. In the name of Jesus Christ our Lord we pray. Amen.

– Captain Marvin E. Snyder, CHC, USN (Ret.)

A PRAYER FOR THE UNITED STATES NAVY

O Lord, our Lord, how great is Your glory throughout all the earth! We call upon our souls, and all that is within us, to praise and bless Your Name. For Your majesty is reflected in all creation. In Your hands are the depth of the sea and the awesome powers of the air. With the eye of faith we observe Your Presence all about us. We thank You, Lord, for the privilege and challenge of serving in the Naval forces of our country; to be the protector, defender, and promoter of the interests and wellbeing of our land. May our mission and purpose serve to promote peace and justice in a world so needful of both. May we fulfil our calling with honour and loyalty, so that Your will may be done on earth through us. For all who sail the oceans and ply its depths and fly its spaces we earnestly seek Your grace and care. May we not fear, for You are our help and our salvation. May we not fail, for You are the strength of our lives. May we not lose courage, knowing that the Eternal God is our refuge and underneath are His everlasting arms. In the Name above all names we pray. Amen.

– Captain Derke P. Bergsma, CHC, USN, (Ret.)

A Deployment Prayer

Almighty God, we turn our thoughts to Thee as we make ready to sail for distant places. Thou knowest the future and will defend us from all adversities both to the soul and body if we will fully trust in Thee. Enable each of us to cheerfully accept his respective place of duty within this ship that we may pass all our days in devotion to our sacred tasks. Watch over our wives, children, and loved ones at home through all the days of our separation, that our return may be a blessed homecoming. Grant us a good ship's spirit, a happy voyage, and a safe return. In Christ's name we pray. Amen.

– Captain Stanford E. Linzey, Jr., CHC, USN (Ret.)

A PRAYER FOR VETERANS

From deep within the American heart comes a burning love of country. Out of that love is born service, a service that may be as minimal as passing loyalty to service that demands the willful giving of one's life. The root of that service is the totality of love....a love that weeps when taps are played, a love that snaps to attention when the flag goes by, a love that reaches a hand to a heart-broken Mother, a love that envelopes a Wounded Warrior, a love that places distinctive honor on men and women who have accepted the call to Active or Reserve service. Grant that the Veterans of our Armed Forces may be brave in battle, high-hearted in hardships, dauntless in defeat, and gentle in victory. Remember our Veterans, for they have trained themselves in peace to help their country in war; and give them skill and courage, endurance and self-control, in the work now set before them. We commend to thy keeping all those who are venturing their lives on our behalf, that whether by life or by death they may win for the whole world the fruits of their sacrifice and a holy peace. Look in thy mercy, Lord, on those who are called to tasks of special peril in the air or beneath the sea. Even there shall thy hand lead them and thy right hand shall hold them. Help them to do their duty with prudence and with fearlessness, confident that in life or in death, thou, Eternal God, art their refuge and underneath are thy everlasting arms. Amen.

– Captain Stanley D. Miller, CHC, USN (Ret.)

A PRAYER FOR ETHICS IN MILITARY LEADERSHIP

God of grace, law, and soundness, Create in me a clear sense, and a moral instinct as pertains to the difficult moral and ethical decisions that I will have to make. May my mind be transformed and my heart changed, so that I will make godly decisions, especially those that have an impact on the troops. May my judgment be crisp, and my heart be sound, to the glory of God. Amen.

– Former Chaplain (CAPTAIN) Michael Pacella, III, USA

THE SINNER'S PRAYER

Dear heavenly Father, I confess that I am a sinner in need of a Saviour. I have been living in sin without You. Without You, my life is empty and depraved. I have followed the sins of my youth, and the sins of my own thinking and actions. I have cared more about myself than of You and others. I believe Jesus Christ is Your only begotten Son. I believe He is God, who came in the flesh. I believe He rose from the dead and in Him, only, is eternal life granted. I earnestly implore you to save me from my sins. Please forgive me for sinning against You, against others, and against my own conscience. Strengthen me to live a holy life. Search my heart, O God. Cleanse my heart from every evil desire. Create in me a clean heart. Renew my spirit. Let me thirst no more. But give me the longing to fulfill Your will and hunger after only righteousness. Lead me to live according to the Scriptures. When I fall, pick me up. Keep me in Your will. Now, fill me with the Holy Spirit. In Jesus' name, I pray. Amen.

APPENDIX D
MILITARY HYMNS

THE AIR FORCE HYMN

Lord, guard and guide the men who fly
Through the great spaces of the sky;
Be with them traversing the air
In darkening storms or sunshine fair

Thou who dost keep with tender might
The balanced birds in all their flight
Thou of the tempered winds be near
That, having thee, they know no fear

Control their minds with instinct fit
What time, adventuring, they quit
The firm security of land;
Grant steadfast eye and skillful hand

Aloft in solitudes of space,
Uphold them with Thy saving grace.
O God, protect the men who fly
Through lonely ways beneath the sky.
Amen.

Verse One by Mary C.D. Hamilton (1915)

THE ARMY SONG

First to fight for the right, and to build the Nation's might,
And the Army goes rolling along.
Proud of all we have done, fighting till the battle's won,
And the Army goes rolling along.

Refrain
Then it's Hi! Hi! Hey! The Army's on its way.
Count off the cadence loud and strong (TWO! THREE!)
For where e'er we go, you will always know
That the Army goes rolling along.

Valley Forge, Custer's ranks, San Juan Hill and Patton's tanks,
And the Army went rolling along
Minute men, from the start, always fighting from the heart,
And the Army keeps rolling along.

(Refrain)

Men in rags, men who froze, still that Army met its foes,
And the Army went rolling along.
Faith in God, then we're right, and we'll fight with all our might,
As the Army keeps rolling along.

(Refrain)

– First Lieutenant Edmund L. Gruber, USA, 1908

THE COAST GUARD HYMN

Eternal Father, Lord of Hosts
Watch o'er the ones who guard our coasts
Protect them from the raging seas
And give them light and life and peace.
Grant them from thy great throne above
The shield and shelter of thy love.
Amen.

– CWO George H. Jenks, Jr., USCG, 1955

THE MARINE CORPS HYMN

From the Halls of Montezuma,
To the shores of Tripoli;
We fight our country's battles
In the air, on land, and sea;
First to fight for right and freedom
And to keep our honor clean;
We are proud to claim the title
Of United States Marine.

Our flag's unfurled to every breeze
From dawn to setting sun;
We have fought in every clime and place
Where we could take a gun;
In the snow of far-off Northern lands
And in sunny tropic scenes;
You will find us always on the job
The United States Marines.

Here's health to you and to our Corps
Which we are proud to serve;
In many a strife we've fought for life
And never lost our nerve;
If the Army and the Navy
Ever look on Heaven's scenes;
They will find the streets are guarded
By United States Marines.

Author Unknown, 19th Century
Music from Gendarmes' Duet from the opera Geneviève de
Brabant
by Jacques Offenbach

THE NAVY HYMN

Eternal Father, strong to save,
Whose arm hath bound the restless wave,
Who bidd'st the mighty ocean deep
Its own appointed limits keep;
Oh, hear us when we cry to Thee,
For those in peril on the sea!

O Christ! Whose voice the waters heard
And hushed their raging at Thy word,
Who walked'st on the foaming deep,
And calm amidst its rage didst sleep;
Oh, hear us when we cry to Thee,
For those in peril on the sea!

Most Holy Spirit! Who didst brood
Upon the chaos dark and rude,
And bid its angry tumult cease,
And give, for wild confusion, peace;
Oh, hear us when we cry to Thee,
For those in peril on the sea!

O Trinity of love and power!
Our brethren shield in danger's hour;
From rock and tempest, fire and foe,
Protect them whereso'er they go.
Thus evermore shall rise to Thee,
Glad praise from air, and land, and sea!

Words by William Whiting (1860)
Music by Rev. John Bacchus Dykes (1861)

OH GLORY BE TO GOD

I found the Christ my Savior sweet;
In Him I do delight.
He is my God and Lord and King,
I love with all my might.

Hallelujah! Hallelujah! Hallelujah!
Oh glory be to God!

He found me when I was in sin;
My heart was black as night.
He cleansed my soul and took me in,
And now I am made right.

Hallelujah! Hallelujah! Hallelujah!
Oh glory be to God!

He hung upon the tree one day;
The Righteous was brought low.
He died to show the sinful world
The way that man most go.

Hallelujah! Hallelujah! Hallelujah!
Oh glory be to God!

The gospel story has been told;
The promise is in store.
He who will obey the Lord
Has life forever more.

Hallelujah! Hallelujah! Hallelujah!
Oh glory be to God!

– Musician First Class Stanford E. Linzey, Jr., USN

Appendix E

The Military Believer's Creed

I believe in God the Father, the Creator of heaven and earth, and in Jesus Christ, His only begotten Son. He was conceived by the Holy Spirit and born of the Virgin Mary. He suffered under Pontius Pilate, was crucified, dead, and buried. He descended into hell. On the third day He rose from the dead. He ascended into heaven and sits at the right hand of God the Father. He will come to judge the living and the dead. I believe in the Holy Spirit, the holy Christian Church, the communion of saints, the forgiveness of sins, the resurrection of the body, and eternal life through Jesus Christ, our Lord and Savior. Amen.

APPENDIX F

The Role of Military Chaplains

by Chaplain (MAJOR), James F. Linzey, ARNG (Ret.)

The military is about training lean, mean fighting machines, but military men and women have their weaknesses. Due to the pressures they've been under, military men and women often forget about discipline during rest and relaxation, and they often do things they regret, leaving indelible scars on their consciences. Airmen, coast guardsmen, marines, sailors, and soldiers have to learn to shore up their moral weaknesses. Military chaplains are there to help strengthen these areas of weakness, to make troops spiritually strong.

The military chaplains are there to strengthen the men and women so that they do not find themselves sitting in the infirmary wondering what happened to them. With the help of the Holy Spirit, military chaplains provide hope in the military community so that military men and women don't need to cling to binges to survive life.

Suicide sometimes occurs in the military and presents another danger military chaplains fight. When young military men and women take their lives, they are lost. Military chaplains provide the Word of God. The Gospel is the power of God unto salvation, now and eternally.

Even atheists rely on chaplains for their therapeutic value. There is something present beyond the natural when military chaplains are involved. Further, chaplains provide privileged communication and confidentiality to all military men and women and their families. This provides essential reinforcement. The men and women in the military are put under extreme pressure, taking other's lives and seeing their buddies blown apart. They fight to protect their country and families and everything they hold dear, and they might even save their own lives in the process. Having a chaplain there to share their burden can make all the difference.

There is another aspect to this as well. The goal in each battle is to come back whole, but this goal is not always attained. In such cases, having had a military chaplain to share the plan of salvation might make an eternal world of difference.

Military men and women need hope so that when they walk onto the battlefield they'll walk back from the battlefield. These are your sons and daughters and your brothers and sisters. Handing out Bibles is a crucial role of military chaplains. But going beyond that and ministering to military men and women from the Bible provides a unified effort to shore up the moral fibre of the military and save lives.

APPENDIX G
Photo Gallery

Captain Stanford E. Linzey, Jr., CHC, USN
Official United States Navy Photo

SAN DIEGO, CALIFORNIA, 1940 — VERNA TOOK STAN TO CHURCH ON
THEIR FIRST DATE, WHICH WAS ON FEBRUARY 11, 1940. SHE SHARED
WITH HIM THE IMPORTANCE OF THE BAPTISM WITH THE HOLY
SPIRIT WHEN THEY DATED AND WHEN HE CAME TO VISIT HER AT
HER PARENTS' HOME. IN 1942, STAN RECEIVED IT. HE WAS THE FIRST
CLARINETIST IN THE NAVY BAND ABOARD THE USS *YORKTOWN* (CV-
5). ALSO, VERNA WAS A PERFORMING CLARINETIST AND A SOPRANO.

JULY 29, 1942 – THIS WAS THE DAY STAN RECEIVED THE BAPTISM WITH
THE HOLY SPIRIT AT RAYMOND HARMS' CHURCH IN LOS ANGELES,
CALIFORNIA. FROM RIGHT TO LEFT: REV. EARL DAVIS, REV. RAYMOND
HARMS, MUSICIAN FIRST CLASS STANFORD E. LINZEY, JR., USN, AND
NELSON E. HINMAN (PHOTO: COURTESY OF VERNA LINZEY).

EVANGEL UNIVERSITY, SPRINGFIELD, MO, NOVEMBER 17-22, 1968 –
STAN, AT THE RANK OF COMMANDER, SPOKE AT EVANGEL UNIVERSITY AS
THE KEYNOTE SPEAKER FOR SPIRITUAL EMPHASIS WEEK, MINISTERING
ON THE BAPTISM WITH THE HOLY SPIRIT. TWENTY-ONE STUDENTS
RECEIVED THE BAPTISM. ABOVE, STAN COUNSELS EVANGEL STUDENT
BOB STONE, OF ST. PAUL MINNESOTA, TO HELP HIM UNDERSTAND THE
DOCTRINE AND RECEIVE THE EXPERIENCE. (PHOTO: COURTESY OF
EVANGEL UNIVERSITY).

EVANGELISTIC CRUSADE, ABOUT 1985 – STAN IS SHOWN LAYING
HANDS ON BELIEVERS DURING THE ALTAR CALL TO RECEIVE THE
BAPTISM WITH THE HOLY SPIRIT. THIS WAS TYPICAL OF THE MEETINGS
WE CONDUCTED. HE WOULD PREACH THE SERIES OF MESSAGES IN THE
BOOK YOUR ARE HOLDING IN YOUR HANDS. AND I WOULD USUALLY
LAY HANDS ON AND PRAY WITH OTHERS DURING THESE ALTAR CALLS.
(PHOTO: COURTESY OF VERNA LINZEY).

GULF OF TONKIN – "HOLY HELO." STAN, AT THE RANK OF CAPTAIN,
IS BEING HOISTED UP TO THE "HOLY HELO" FROM THE DECK OF A
"SMALL BOY" – A NAVY DESTROYER – IN THE GULF OF TONKIN DURING
THE VIET NAM WAR. DURING THIS TOUR OF DUTY, THE CORAL SEA
WAS DUBBED THE PENTECOSTAL SHIP DUE TO A PENTECOSTAL REVIVAL
THAT BROKE OUT RESULTING IN ABOUT 100 SEAMEN RECEIVING THE
BAPTISM WITH THE HOLY SPIRIT. THREE WERE ROMAN CATHOLIC
SAILORS WHO LATER BECAME PENTECOSTAL CHAPLAINS IN THE AIR
FORCE, ARMY AND NAVY (U.S. NAVY PHOTO).

SAN DIEGO, CALIFORNIA – STAN, AS A RETIRED CAPTAIN AND WWII
VETERAN, DELIVERED THE INVOCATION BEHIND THE SEAL OF THE
PRESIDENT OF THE UNITED STATES ON AUGUST 28, 2005, BEFORE
PRESIDENT GEORGE W. BUSH SPOKE. THE EVENT WAS THE 60TH
ANNIVERSARY OF JAPAN'S SURRENDER IN WORLD WAR II. THIS
CEREMONY OCCURRED AT NAVAL BASE CORONADO, SAN DIEGO,
CALIFORNIA (PHOTO: COURTESY OF CHAPLAIN JIM LINZEY).

VERNA LINZEY, D.D.

About the Author

CAPTAIN STANFORD E. LINZEY, JR., CHC, USN (RET.) was the founder of Holy Spirit Evangelism. He was a retired United States Navy Chaplain having served for over 28 years of active service, initially as an enlisted sailor and then as an officer. He began his military career in the United States Navy in 1939. When he enlisted in the Navy he was selected to attend the United States Navy School of Music in Washington, D.C. He served as an enlisted musician from 1939 to 1947. He served on the ill-fated aircraft carrier, USS *Yorktown* (CV-5), which fought in the Battle of the Coral Sea, and which was later sunk by the Japanese in the Battle of Midway in June 1942. He was aboard when it was bombed, torpedoed and began to sink. In 1947, he left the Navy to build and pastor churches, with his wife Verna Linzey, and receive higher education to prepare to qualify for the United States Navy Chaplain Corps.

On July 1, 1955, Rev. Linzey was accepted into the Chaplain Corps with the rank of Lieutenant, Junior Grade. He was promoted to the rank of Captain on July 1, 1972. He was the first Assemblies of God Chaplain in the regular Navy and the first chaplain from his church to attain the rank of Captain.

Among Chaplain Linzey's assignments as a chaplain, he served with 7th Marine Regiment – 1st Marine Division, Camp

Pendleton, California, 1955-56; 12th Marine Regiment – 3rd Marine Division, Okinawa, 1956-57; Naval Training Center – San Diego, California, 1957-59; Destroyer Squadron Five, 1959-61; Naval Air Station, Imperial Beach, California, 1961-62; USS *Holland* (AS-32), 1963-64; U.S. Naval Station, San Diego, California, 1964-68; USS *Galveston* (CLG-3), 1966-68; U.S. Naval Air Station, Moffett Field, California, 1968-70; USS *Coral Sea* (CVA-43), Command Chaplain, 1971-73; U.S. Naval Air Station, Moffett Field, California, 1973-74. Captain Linzey retired from the Naval Service on September 30, 1974.

Chaplain Linzey has traveled extensively throughout North America, Europe and the world ministering and speaking on subjects relating to the work of the Holy Spirit in the New Testament Age. He has toured the Far East many times, ministering in Korea, Okinawa, Philippines, Japan, Hong Kong and Singapore. He was sought after speaker in the churches, colleges, civic organizations, and men's fellowship groups. The ministry of this charismatic lecturer and minister has touched thousands.

Chaplain Linzey received the B.A., Th.B. and Doctor of Divinity degrees from Southern California Seminary, El Cajon, California; a Master of Divinity degree from American Baptist Seminary of the West, Berkeley, California; studied at Harvard Divinity School, Cambridge, Massachusetts, as a resident graduate; and received a Doctor of Ministry Degree from Fuller Theological Seminary, Pasadena, California.

Chaplain Linzey is listed in *Who's Who in Religion, International Men of Achievement*, and *5000 Personalities of the World*.

Chaplain and Mrs. Linzey had 10 children: Gena English, Jan Mathis, Eugene Linzey, Darnell Lemons, Sharon Linzey, George Linzey, Vera Clark, Paul Linzey, Dave Linzey, and Jim Linzey.

Chaplain Linzey received his final promotion when he went to be with the Lord on February 4, 2010.

CPSIA information can be obtained at www.ICGtesting.com
Printed in the USA
BVOW010807081112

304860BV00002B/6/P